Essential
Ibiza
& Formentera

by Richard Sale

Richard Sale took up writing full time
after spending many years as a research
scientist. He has contributed to a
number of magazines, chiefly on outdoor
topics, and of the 25 or so books he has
had published, most are travel guides to
European destinations.
Richard lives on the Cotswold Way in
Gloucestershire.

AA Publishing

Above: *a window in one of Balafia's ancient houses*

Page 1: *Portinatx*

Page 5: *woman in traditional dress*

Page15a: *Jesús*
15b: *within the church of Puig de Missa*

Page 27: *Es Cubells*

Page 91: *accessories for the beach in Sant Antoni*

Page 117: *souvenir shop, Ibiza*

Find out more about AA Publishing and the wide range of services the AA provides by visiting our Web site at www.theaa.co.uk

Written by Richard Sale

Edited, designed and produced by AA Publishing.
© The Automobile Association 1998
Maps © The Automobile Association 1998

Distributed in the United Kingdom by AA Publishing, Norfolk House, Priestley Road, Basingstoke, Hampshire, RG24 9NY.

A CIP catalogue record for this book is available from the British Library.

ISBN 0 7495 1630 5

The contents of this publication are believed correct at the time of printing. Nevertheless, the publishers cannot be held responsible for any errors or omissions or for changes in the details given in this guide or for the consequences of any reliance on the information provided by the same. Assessments of attractions, hotels, restaurants and so forth are based upon the author's own experience and, therefore, descriptions given in this guide necessarily contain an element of subjective opinion which may not reflect the publisher's opinion or dictate a reader's own experience on another occasion.

We have tried to ensure accuracy in this guide, but things do change and we would be grateful if readers would advise us of any inaccuracies they may encounter.

Published by AA Publishing, a trading name of Automobile Association Developments Limited, whose registered office is Norfolk House, Priestley Road, Basingstoke, Hampshire, RG24 9NY.
Registered number 1878835.

Colour separation: BTB Digital Imaging, Whitchurch, Hampshire

Printed and bound in Italy by Printers Trento srl

Contents

About this Book

Essential *Ibiza & Formentera* is divided into five sections to cover the most important aspects of your visit.

Viewing Ibiza & Formentera pages 5–14
An introduction to the islands by the author.
Ibiza & Formentera's Features
Essence of Ibiza & Formentera
The Shaping of the Pine Islands
Peace and Quiet
Ibiza & Formentera's Famous

Top Ten pages 15–26
The author's choice of the Top Ten places to visit in Ibiza & Formentera, each with practical information.

What to See pages 27–90
The islands of Ibiza & Formentera, each with its own brief introduction and an alphabetical listing of the main attractions.
Practical information
Snippets of 'Did You Know...' information
4 suggested tours, 5 suggested walks
2 features

Where To... pages 91–116
Detailed listings of the best places to eat, stay, shop, take the children and be entertained.

Practical Matters pages 117–24
A highly visual section containing essential travel information.

Maps
All map references are to the individual maps found in the What to See section of this guide.
For example, Dalt Vila has the reference ✚ 33D2 – indicating the page on which the map is located and the grid square in which the medieval town is to be found.
A list of the maps that have been used in this travel guide can be found in the index.

Prices
Where appropriate, an indication of the cost of an establishment is given by £ signs:
£££ denotes higher prices, **££** denotes average prices, while **£** denotes lower charges.

Star Ratings
Most of the places described in this book have been given a separate rating:

😮😮😮	Do not miss
😮😮	Highly recommended
😮	Worth seeing

Viewing
Ibiza
& Formentera

Richard Sale's Ibiza & Formentera

Calm and Efficient

It is no surprise that *mañana* is a Spanish word; it might have been invented to describe the relaxed attitude to life of the islanders of Ibiza and Formentera. But do not be entirely deceived. When there is a need to get things done the islanders will respond: buses and ferries run to time, and in restaurants your meal will arrive in good time. The time to relax is after you have finished eating, as you watch the world go by.

Aptly Named

It was the Greeks who first named Ibiza and Formentera, calling them the *Pitiusas*, the Pine Islands, but Ibiza, fittingly perhaps, is named for the Carthaginian god Bes.

Dalt Vila makes an impressive backdrop to a stroll in La Marina, Eivissa

It would be easy to dismiss Ibiza as a holiday destination because of the stories of excesses that follow mass tourism, and it would be foolish to deny that in high summer some places on the island offer a slice of life that is not everyone's cup of tea. Or should that be pint of lager? But despite its small size, Ibiza is large enough to allow travellers to escape both the crowds and their prejudices. The real Ibiza is a marvellous place, a mix of European and North African cultures in a Mediterranean setting.

Emerging from the dark days of Franco's regime when regional characteristics were suppressed in favour of a Castillian Spain, Ibiza has seen a resurgence in Catalan, of which the islanders' language is a dialect. Catalan signs have sprung up and the displays in museums are in Catalan as well as Castillian. Traditional costume, music and dancing survived under Franco, but there seems a new vitality in them now.

Ibizan history is one of conquest and settlement – the Phoenicians, the Greeks, the Carthaginians, the Moors and the Catalans each leaving their mark on the island. The Carthaginian remains are among the finest in the world, while the rural architecture reflects North African traditions as strongly as European. And there was another effect. The islands developed a live-and-let-live attitude to newcomers that is still a feature, and a welcome one, of today's island.

Ibiza & Formentera's Features

Geographical Information

Ibiza
• Area: 570sq km.
• Highest Point: Sa Talaia, at 475m.
• Longest River: Rio de Santa Eulària. The river is 11km long and is the only river not only on Ibiza but on the Balearic Islands. Santa Eulària des Riu is therefore the only Balearic town that stands on a river.
• Length of coastline: 210km.
• Population: about 80,000, of whom 30,000 live in Eivissa.
• Ibiza lies about 80km from mainland Spain.

Formentera
• Area: 80sq km.
• Highest Point: La Mola at 192m.
• Length: Formentera is only 19km from end to end.
• Population: about 5,000.
• Formentera lies about 220km from North Africa.

Climate
• On average, Ibiza and Formentera have 300 days of sunshine each year. In summer there is an average of 10 hours' sunshine every day.
• In all months the average sea temperature is warmer than the average air temperature.

Economic Factors
Ibiza and Formentera are famous for:
• Tourism. In summer there are four tourists for every native islander.
• Hippies, but these have now grown old and respectable (more or less).
• Nude bathing, which is practised with enthusiasm on many beaches.
• Potteries: on Formentera look for pieces with a lizard motif.
• Leatherware: a centuries-old traditional craft.
• Art galleries, because the light and climate attract artists.
• Ad Lib fashion, a new local craft, dating from the hippy invasion of the 1960s.

Sport and Leisure
• Anything to do with water.
• Walking.
• Cycling.
• Tennis.

Taking to the water at Platja d'en Bossa

Essence of Ibiza & Formentera

If you have only a limited time on the Pine Islands you will need to be as careful in what you avoid as what you see. The holiday islands are the beaches and the new developments that back them. These places have a vitality that is impressive, but you have to be part of the crowd if you are truly to enjoy them. The real islands are quieter and to explore those you will need to head away from the teeming beaches, going along the coast to more secluded coves or heading inland to villages seemingly as untouched by mass tourism as they have been by the procession of armies that have passed this way.

In many inland areas, Ibizan women still wear traditional dress

THE **10** ESSENTIALS

If you only have a short time to visit Ibiza and Formentera, or would like to get a really complete picture of the islands, here are the essentials:

• **Take a walk** around Dalt Vila (➤ 20). Before you start, it might be an idea to buy some *espadrilles*, the traditional Spanish rope-soled sandals. The whole history of the Pine Islands is set out in Eivissa's upper town.

• **Find a quiet section of coast** and go for a walk. Near Cap de Barbaría, on Formentera, you can gaze out across the Mediterranean in the direction of Africa and imagine you are a Moor looking towards home.

• **Take a boat trip** around a part of the islands' coast and try to understand how it must have felt to see the islands for the first time.

• **Find a quiet inland village** on Ibiza and stroll around. Admire the distinctive architecture and relax, the way the locals do.

• **Join in a *ball páge*,** the traditional island festival with music and singing; discover that the locals do occasionally let their hair down.

• **Buy a drink or a meal at El Corsario,** Dalt Vila's most famous hotel/restaurant.

• **Go for a swim.** No visit would be complete without a dip in the clear, warm waters. If you really want to swim in style, take off all your clothes at one of the official nudist beaches.

• **Eat fresh fish** at a beach restaurant. The islands are famous for their fish dishes and sometimes you can watch the fish you are going to eat being caught.

• **Take a stroll through La Marina** in Eivissa to watch the comings and goings of the younger visitors as they seek out the latest Ad Lib fashions.

• **On your last night take a glass of sangria** to a cliff top on the western side of the island and watch the sun setting over the Mediterranean.

The elaborate entrance portal to the cathedral in Eivissa

9

The Shaping of the Pine Islands

2000 BC
First settlement by hunter-gatherers/fishermen from mainland Spain. Ca'na Costa on Formentera, the islands' most important prehistoric site, dates from this period.

700 BC
Phoenicians settle on Ibiza, building settlements at Sa Caleta and Eivissa, though Sa Caleta is abandoned after about 40 years.

654 BC
The official date of the settlement of Ibiza by the Carthaginians. A mint is built at Eivissa, producing coins featuring the god Bes, who gives his name to the island.

202 BC
Rome defeats Carthage in the Second Punic War, but Ibiza escapes conquest.

146 BC
The fall of Carthage. Ibiza becomes a confederate state of Rome, but is neither conquered nor fully occupied, its inhabitants retaining their Carthaginian traditions, though the coins from the mint now have the heads of Roman Emperors on them.

AD 426
With the fall of Rome, the islands are unprotected and are conquered by the Vandals.

535
The Vandals are defeated by Count Belisario, who takes Ibiza for the Byzantine Empire.

902
After several centuries of raids by the Moors of North Africa, Ibiza and Formentera are finally taken permanently, becoming, at first, part of Cordoban Caliphate and, later, part of the Moorish kingdom of Mallorca.

1114
Pisa launches a crusade against Ibiza, sending a huge fleet to the island. After weeks of siege the Pisans are successful, but only plunder the island before retreating. However, Moorish rule of Ibiza is seriously weakened and within a little over a century comes to an end.

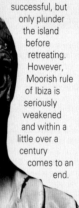

The great Carthaginian general Hannibal, who is said to have been born on Ibiza

1235
On 8 August Archbishop Guillem de Montgri takes Ibiza on behalf of King Jaime I of Aragon. Christianity replaces Islam as the island's religion.

1276–1342
Ibiza and Formentera form part of the kingdom of Mallorca.

Late 14th–late 18th centuries
Ibiza and Formentera become a backwater in tidal surges of European power politics. During this period Christopher Columbus discovers America and Spain forgets the islands in its enthusiasm for empire building.

During the 16th and 17th centuries the Corsairs of the Barbary Coast attack Ibiza frequently, resulting in the building of coastal watchtowers and fortified churches. Ibiza eventually retaliates with its own fleets, who are very successful. Finally the Napoleonic Wars lead to a strengthening of Europe's Mediterranean coast and an end to pirate raids. In 1662 plague strikes Ibiza, killing a good proportion of the population.

1815–1936
After the Napoleonic Wars life on Ibiza and Formentera, aided by

Eivissa's formidable walls were built in the 16th century to fend off pirates

the lack of piracy, become quiet and peaceful, a peace shattered in 1936 by the Spanish Civil War.

1960s
Cheaper air travel – in part due to large-capacity jets – brings mass tourism to the islands with a rush of building.

1975
General Franco dies. Democracy returns to Spain and King Juan

Carlos I is restored as monarch.

1983
Ibiza and Formentera become part of the Communitat Autonoma de les Illes Balears.

1986
Spain joins the European Community (now the European Union).

1991
An Act of Parliament is set up to protect the natural environment.

1994
The King and Queen of Spain make their first official visit to the Pine Islands.

Peace & Quiet

With mass tourism filling several of the towns and most of the beaches it could easily be assumed that peace and quiet were the hardest things to find on Ibiza. In fact it could not be easier – just walk away from a crowded beach for a few minutes and you will be on a deserted section of coast, or drive for a few miles from any town and you will be in countryside that seems to have been untouched by time.

Above: *the yellow-legged gull is one of the islands' rarer seabirds*
Below: *though often seen, goats are not native to the Pine Islands*

Around the Coast

On Ibiza, and even more so on Formentera, wild flowers can be found clinging precariously to life in rocky crevices and other unlikely places. On the beaches and in the backing sand dunes there are sea daffodils and sea holly, but also some much rarer plants. The islands are the only place in Europe where a particular form of squill (*Scilla numidica*) grows, and the only place in the world where *Silene cambessedesii* (a delicate and very beautiful campion) is found.

In the remaining wooded areas behind the dunes – the woodland chiefly Aleppo pine – those willing to spend time exploring will find many types of orchids. Mirror orchid, with blue flowers edged with brown, is relatively common, as is the sombre bee orchid (*Ophrys fusca*). By contrast, the bee orchid (*Ophrys apifera*) is rare and endangered.

The Mediterranean is home to surprisingly few seabirds and waders. The lack of tides and, therefore, an intertidal region, discourages wading birds, while the sea's warm waters are less densely packed with food than the colder waters of northern Europe. Nevertheless, the yellow-legged gull will be easily recognised. However, if the gull you are watching has dark legs and a red beak with a yellow tip, then you could have an Audouin's gull in view, claimed to be the rarest gull in the world.

Some specialities

The rarest animal on the islands is the genet, but visitors are extremely unlikely to see one. What they will see are lizards. There are some 40 different types, all sub-species of Podarcis pityusensis, the harmless Ibizan wall lizard. Of the birdlife, the most common 'non-northern' species is the Sardinian warbler, but most visitors will be trying to catch sight of the exotic hoopoe, or the rare Eleonora's falcon (➤ 77).

Unspoilt Hinterland

Formentera is almost too small to have an 'inland' area, but inland Ibiza is a real contrast to the crowded beaches. Here you will be able to find real peace and quiet and fascinating flora and fauna. At almost any time of year inland Ibiza is colourful. In February, January's yellow mimosa is replaced by pink and white almond blossom, and bunch-flowered narcissus. In March, spring arrives, heralded by lavender, rock roses, moon daises and the surprisingly beautiful yellow flowers of the prickly pear cactus. In summer, the bougainvillaea, oleander and honeysuckle are brilliant against the blue of the sky, while the arrival of autumn brings violets, narcissi and squills. The winter months see the heathers blooming and then the bright fruits of the citrus trees.

Above: *mirror orchids, one of Ibiza's most common orchids*
Below: *the spiny leaves of plants such as this thistle afford protection for snails against predators*

13

Ibiza & Formentera's Famous

Cube upon Cube
Le Corbusier, the famous French architect usually said to have been the father of high-rise living, is believed to have found the inspiration for his tower blocks in the simple cube houses of Ibiza and the Ibizan method of increasing space by merely adding more cubes.

Above: *Charles Le Corbusier, 1887–1965*
Right: *the statue of Joaquim Vara de Rey stands in an Eivissa street which also bears his name*

Antonio Riquer
Antonio Riquer was the most famous of Ibiza's Corsairs – a vigilante sea captain or a pirate, depending upon your point of view. His most famous action was the defeat of a feared Gibraltarian pirate called Miguel Novelli, who was nicknamed 'The Pope'. Riquer intercepted 'The Pope' as he was sailing from Formentera to attack Ibiza. Despite having a much smaller ship and being completely outgunned, Riquer's superior seamanship won the day, 'The Pope' breaking off the battle and fleeing just before his ship was about to be boarded or sunk. Riquer is remembered in a street name near Eivissa's harbour, his house in Dalt Vila is on the tourist route, and he was one of the main reasons the Ibizencos raised El Obelisco a los Corsarios, the monument to the Corsairs on La Marina's sea front.

Hannibal
Although the Carthaginians probably originated in what is now Lebanon and had an empire which was virtually confined to the North African coast, they did colonise Ibiza. Legend has it that it was on Sa Conillera, the now uninhabited island lying off Ibiza's western shore, near Sant Antoni, that Hannibal, the most glorious Carthaginian general, was born.

Hannibal is chiefly famous for crossing the Alps with his elephants to defeat Rome, but as important to him as his elephants were the lead pellets fired by his army's slingers. These pellets were formed from lead that had been mined on Ibiza.

Joaquim Vara de Rey
Close to the Tourist Information Office in Paseo Vara de Rey is a statue of the man for whom the street is named. The General is Ibiza's most famous soldier. He died in 1898 defending Cuba, one of Spain's last American colonies, against an invading US army.

14

Top Ten

1
Balafia

🕆 29D4

✉ Close to the Eivissa–Portinatx road

🍴 Ca-na Pepeta (£), on the main road

🚌 Eivissa–Portinatx bus

♿ None

✋ Free

The church of Sant Llorenç stands close to the ancient village of Balafia

> *Nowhere is the Moorish heritage of Ibiza more obvious than in this delightful village.*

Situated off the main road from Eivissa to Portinatx, close to Sant Llorenç and beneath the shapely mass of Es Fornás, Ibiza's third highest peak, Balafia's first claim to a Moorish heritage is its name; it is one of the few on the island that survives from the time before the Christian invasion. The name means 'good water', the village having been sited near a spring of sweet water.

Access to Balafia is via a very narrow rough track, opposite the turn to Sant Carles/Es Canar and the Ca-na Pepeta restaurant. The village, consisting of just seven houses, is a wonderfully evocative place. As you walk around it feels as though you have not only shed several centuries, but also changed continents: Balafia is a small part of Africa deposited here on the outskirts of Europe.

The houses are probably the oldest on the island and follow the traditional design – square-walled and floored, the walls brightly whitewashed and flat-roofed with windows that let in the air but keep out the sun. They are grouped around two squat towers, similar to those found along Ibiza's coastline. When the invading pirates, not content with raiding the coastal villages, swept inland the Balafia villagers retreated to these towers in the hope that the marauders would move on before the towers' stores of food and water ran out. See also ➤ 42.

2
Catedral

The cathedral stands on one of the holiest sites of Ibiza: there was a Moorish mosque here and, prior to that, a Roman temple.

It is speculated that the Romans chose the site because a Carthaginian temple occupied it, the newcomers wanting to replace all aspects of the older culture. If there was indeed a Carthaginian temple then the site has a history of worship going back 2,500 years at least. With the ousting of the Moors, a fine Gothic-style cathedral was built. The construction took a long time, starting in the late 13th century and continuing for 300 years. Of that original church only the apse and the bell-tower – the tower looking very much like an Italian campanile – remain. The rest was pulled down and rebuilt in unimaginative style in the 18th century.

Inside there are a few interesting works of art, but the better pieces have been removed to the cathedral museum which is attached to the main building. One of the best exhibits here is a silver monstrance plate (the 'dish' used to hold the Host at Roman Catholic masses) made in Mallorca in the 15th century. Look, too, for the altarpiece of Sant Macià by a 15th-century Tarragonian master.

One interesting feature of the cathedral is its dedication, which is to the island's patron saint. No surprise there, but in this warmest of European islands the patron saint is Santa Maria de las Neus, the Virgin of the Snows. The reason is that in the calendar of Spanish holy days that of the Virgin of the Snows fell closest to when the Christians captured the island from the Moors.

✚ 33E2

✉ Plaça Catedral, Dalt Vila

🕐 Cathedral and museum: daily 10–1

🍴 The Plaza del Sol (££), Plaça del Sol, close to the Baluarte des Portal Nou

🚌 Not on a bus route

♿ None

✋ Cheap

↔ Archaeological Museum (➤ 36)

❓ There is a sign on the door of the cathedral noting 'When you don't have the right clothes, don't come in'

The distinctive windows of the apse and the Italianate campanile of the cathedral tower above the old houses of Dalt Vila

3
Cala d'Hort

✚ 28A2

✉ At the southwestern tip of the island

🍴 The Cala d'Hort (£), at the beach, or the Es Boldado (££), reached by a stiff walk or by a rough track from the Cala Vadella road

🚌 Not on a bus route, but many resorts organise coach travel

♿ Few

✋ Free

Tucked into a sheltered fold on Ibiza's southeastern coast, Cala d'Hort is one of the island's loveliest bays.

A *cala* is a small bay, of which there are scores dotted around the rugged coast of Ibiza. Many of these bays are quite beautiful, so to qualify as the best of these it follows that Cala d'Hort must be something very special. And indeed it is.

To reach the bay, turn off the main road from Es Cubells to Sant Josep, or that from Sant Josep to Cala Vadella. Until recently the approach road was gravel, but it has now been surfaced and gives speedy access.

Cala d'Hort is exquisite, its 200m beach framed by rocks and with a backdrop of steep cliffs and pine trees. If possible, try to stay until sunset: Cala d'Hort faces west and the sun dying into the Mediterranean horizon is another reason for the bay's popularity. The view from the cliff-top car park above the bay's southern end is magnificent.

Of course you will not have the bay to yourself; nothing this idyllic could remain a secret. Popularity has brought development and, as elsewhere on the island, it has not always been as sympathetic as it might have been – though the facilities do mean that all visitors, from the energetic to those looking for a relaxing day, are well served.

For lunch you can try the bay's restaurants. The fish dishes are worth considering: if you watch closely you will see the fish being caught from the beach, making it as fresh as it is possible to be.

Off-shore to the south, beyond the rounded headland of Cap Blanc, are the photogenic islands of Es Vedrá (►55) and Es Vendranell.

Left: *from Cala d'Hort there is an impressive view of Es Vedrá*

Below: *looking north along Cala d'Hort*

4
Dalt Vila

33D2

The old town of Eivissa

The Plaza del Sol (££), in the Plaça del Sol close to the Baluarte des Portal Nou

Not on a bus route; just a short walk from Eivissa's harbour

Few

Free

Dominating any view of Eivissa, Ibiza's capital, is Dalt Vila, a marvellous medieval town still encircled by its old walls.

Dalt Vila's walls are one of Europe's finest examples of medieval military architecture, so good that they have been declared a Spanish National Monument and their restoration is being funded, in part, by the European Union. Within them, and in the narrow streets of the town below, you will experience a sense of the history of Ibiza.

The walls date from the 16th century, when Carlos (Charles) V decided to reinforce the island's defences against Turkish pirates and the threat they represented of a new Saracen invasion. Charles called in Juan Calvi, the Italian military engineer who had already completed new defences at Mallorca and Barcelona. But though Calvi was responsible for the original design, legend has it that his local foreman, a man known only as *El Fratin*, changed the plan frequently, expanding the defences and creating most of what we see today. Around the walls there are seven *baluartes* (bastions) on which artillery was mounted.

Within the walls are some of Ibiza's most interesting sites, and some of its most entertaining streets: any walk is worthwhile, and in almost every square – sometimes, it seems, on every corner – there is an atmospheric bar or café.

Here, too, are the best of Ibiza's museums, exploring the history of the island. The Museum of Contemporary Art (► 36) houses the best of present-day work, but there are several commercial galleries, each of which could be showing the work of tomorrow's masters.

Eivissa's cathedral stands at the top of Dalt Vila

5
Jesús

In the pretty hamlet of Jesús, close to Eivissa, stands one of Ibiza's most charming churches, home to the island's greatest art treasure.

To many visitors staying in Eivissa, Jesús is just another village on the road to the beaches of Talamanca or Cala Llonga. It is a pretty little place – though somewhat spoiled by the main road running through it – yet not really pretty enough to distinguish it from many another on the island. Until, that is, you reach the church.

The church is a magnificent building, beautifully arcaded on one side and with the typically austere Romanesque-style frontage popular in 15th-century Spain. The solidness of the construction owes much to its history, such village churches having been built by the villagers themselves rather than by craft builders, each man lending his own particular skills and style. The church also often served as a refuge during pirate attacks.

It is not, however, for the exterior that the church is famous. Inside is the island's greatest work of art, the retable, or altar screen. This triptych, a three-panelled painting, is thought to have been completed early in the 16th century by the Valencian artist Rodrigo de Osona. The base of the retable shows the seven key events in the life of the Virgin from the Annunciation to the Assumption. Above is the Virgin and Child, a work of intimacy and gentleness, quite different in character from the more formal poses that are normally seen in paintings of the period. Above is St Francis of Assisi receiving the stigmata. Above again is Christ appearing to St Gregory. The side panels of the triptych show further scenes from the lives of the saints.

The church is usually locked, but the key can sometimes be obtained from the nearby bar/restaurant, Bon Lloc. Alternatively, the retable can be viewed before or after services. See also ➤ 52.

✝ 28C3

✉ Just off the Eivissa–Cala Llonga road

🍴 Bon Lloc (££), close to the church

🚌 Eivissa–Santa Eulària bus

♿ Good

✋ Free

The Virgin and Child *from the retable in the church at Jesús*

6
La Mola, Formentera

✝ 29F1

✉ The extreme eastern end of Formentera

🍴 Es Puig (£), at the end of the road, near the lighthouse

🚌 Sant Ferran–La Mola

♿ None

✋ Free

For rugged grandeur, there is nothing that compares with the rocks of Formentera's Cap de la Mola headland.

From Sant Françesc, Formentera's 'capital', three roads head off for the island's coasts. One reaches La Savina, the port for Ibiza, another heads for Cap de Barbaria, and the third for the eastern headland of La Mola. The latter ends at the La Mola lighthouse, built to warn seafarers of the dangerous rocks that lie below it. The rock of the high plateau of Formentera's eastern tip is exposed here, the limestone forming a pavement of huge flat slabs. Windblown soil has gathered in the gaps between the slabs and hardy plants have rooted, making the area an interesting spot for the botanist. Walk cautiously across the pavement towards the cliff's edge – the cracks between the rock slabs can trip the unwary and there is a sheer drop. Please be especially careful if you have children with you.

The view from the headland is magnificent, the rocks themselves – in shades of red and grey – being particularly picturesque against the turquoise sea. On clear days Mallorca is visible away to the northeast.

The lighthouse at La Mola was built in 1861 by Emilio Pou. First lit by vegetable oil, it had a range of about 55km. The fuel was changed from oil to paraffin and then to petrol and finally to electricity when Formentera was electrified in the 1960s. Interestingly, the upgrading of the light to modern power has meant only a modest increase in range, to 65km. Unfortunately the lighthouse can only be seen from the outside as it is not open to the public. See also ➤ 87.

The dramatic cliffs at La Mola

7

Las Salinas, Formentera

Whereas the salt pans on Ibiza are intensively worked, those on Formentera have largely been given back to the island's wildlife.

The islands' *salinas*, pools for the extraction of salt, have been prized since man first inhabited Ibiza and Formentera, the salt being used to preserve food on long sea voyages. Because of this valuable commodity trading nations were keen to acquire the islands, thus explaining the interest of the Phoenicians, Greeks and Carthaginians.

Salt is still a major industry on Ibiza, but production is much less intensive on Formentera today and the salt lagoons of Estany des Peix and Estany Pudent are now largely the preserve of wildlife, the curious mix of sandy shoreline and dunes and the expanses of high-salinity water supporting a varied collection of plant life and a number of exotic birds. The lakes are also strangely beautiful, with patches of oddly coloured water and a fringe of old salt heaps.

Estany Pudent (the name means 'smelly lagoon' – very appropriate when low water levels expose weeds which quickly rot in the burning sun) is the best place for bird-watchers, over 250 species of birds having been recorded there. Several use the lagoon as a stop-over, but there are resident colonies of egrets, stints, herons and other waders. For many visitors, however, the main attraction is the flocks of flamingos which arrive in late summer. See also ➤ 87.

✚ 29E2

✉ Estany des Peix and Estany Pudent lie each side of the La Savina–Sant Françesc road

🍴 None close to the lagoons, but many in the nearby towns of Es Pujols, Sant Françesc & La Savina, for example the Casa Rafael (££), ✉ 14 Carrer d'Isidor Macabich, Sant Françesc

🚌 Es Pujols–Sant Françesc–La Savina

♿ None

✋ Free

Sunset over Las Salinas, on the northern tip of the island

8
Puig de Missa

Statue inside the church on Puig de Missa (below)

On the outskirts of Santa Eulària stands a hill hich, though only 100m high, offers outstanding views of the island.

t between the town of Santa Eulària des Riu (Santa lalia del Rio) and the river of the same name is the Puig Missa, a shallow hill reached by Avenida Padre Guasch, ich leaves the main road into town just beyond the river ige. At the top is a church dedicated to the saint of the town's name. Dating from the 16th century, the church has a somewhat mysterious origin although the accepted wisdom is that it replaced one destroyed at around that time by Turkish raiders.

Whatever its origins the church was built, as was often the case on the island, to act as a refuge in times of pirate attack. However, its design is far more complex than that of most other island churches. Indeed, after Eivissa's cathedral it is the most architecturally extravagant church on Ibiza. In addition, both its setting and views are superb. The cemetery beside the church is worth a visit for its quiet dignity, while the nearby houses – set out like chicks around a mother hen – are the familiar white Ibizan cubes.

Below the church is the **Museo Etnològic d'Eivissa i Formentera**, set up in 1994 in Can Ros, one of the Puig's older houses. The restored house contains clothing and jewellery, plus various bygones. See also ➤ 61.

✝ 29D4

✉ Puig de Missa: take Avenida Padre Guasch, off the Eivissa–Santa Eulària road

🍴 La Posada (££), a fine, palm-fringed restaurant signed from Avenida Padre Guasch

🚌 Eivissa–Santa Eulària; the bus does not go right to the top of the hill

♿ None

✊ Free

Museo Etnològic d'Eivissa i Formentera

✉ Puig de Missa, below the church

☎ 33 28 45

🕐 May–Sep 11–1, 5–8; Oct–Apr 11–1, 4–7. Closed Sun and Mon morning

🍴 La Posada, as above

🚌 See above

♿ None

✊ Cheap

9
Sant Carles

The beautiful little town of Sant Carles de Peralta is set among some of Ibiza's most idyllic scenery.

The area around Sant Carles (San Carlos) is almost a study in contrasts. To the south, close to the road, is a collection of ruinous buildings and tall cylindrical chimneys, the remains of old lead mines first dug by the Carthaginians.

Closer to the town, the rich red earth, wonderfully fertile despite the relative lack of water, is intensively farmed. In Sant Carles itself, the region's market town, the centrepiece is the church. Built in the 18th century, it is more graceful than many others on the island and has a beautiful double-arcaded entrance. At first glance it could be mistaken for an elegant country house: only when the simple bell housing and cross on the roof are seen does the building's true nature become clear. Inside, the Stations of the Cross – usually displayed on the walls of the Pine Islands' churches – are in carved wood.

During the 1960s Ibiza was 'invaded' by hippies who set up market stalls at places on the coast close to Sant Carles. As time passed many of the hippies migrated inland, some arriving in the town. Their wilder days over, some have settled down, adding a vitality (there are several boutiques and good cafés) to the town which make a visit even more enjoyable. See also ➤ 69.

✝ 29D4

✉ On the main road from Santa Eulària to the northeastern tip of the island

🍴 Peralta (£), a modern bar/restaurant with a beautiful patio overlooking the church

🚌 Santa Eulària–Es Figueral

♿ Few

✋ Free

Sant Carles, inland from the busier coast, is ideal for a quiet, relaxing drink

10
Santa Eulària des Riu

✝ 29D3

✉ On Ibiza's eastern coast a few kilometres north of Eivissa

🍴 Pizzeria Magu, towards the harbour end of the seafront

🚌 Santa Eulària is served by buses from all parts of the island

♿ Few

✋ Free

Ibiza's third largest town, rare in that it has been extended for the benefit of the tourist industry without losing its charm.

Santa Eulària des Riu (or Santa Eulalia del Rio) is the only town in the Balearics to be set on a river. The townsfolk's pride in their unique setting is reflected in the addition to the name, though it must be said that the river is barely more than a stream and in summer often dries to little more than a trickle between pools. Both river and town are named for the saint to whom the church on nearby Puig de Missa (➤ 24) is dedicated.

Santa Eulària grew up as a market town for the local area, a fertile plain well-watered by the river despite its lack of stature. Reflecting this past, the town still has an old quarter with narrow alleys and whitewashed houses, each with a characteristic A-shaped chimney. But Santa Eulària was also one of the first places on Ibiza to attract foreign visitors, a fact which accounts for the modern seafront and harbour. The development of both these areas has been thoughtful, the buildings being architecturally interesting as well as reflecting the prosperity tourism has brought to the town. No building is so avant-garde as to throw the entire area into confusion, as a result of which a stroll along the seafront is fascinating.

At the northern end of the front is the harbour, filled with rows of expensive boats, its jetties lined with shops, excellent restaurants and delightful bars and cafés in which to while away an hour or two. See also ➤ 69.

One of the pleasant squares in the new part of town

What To See

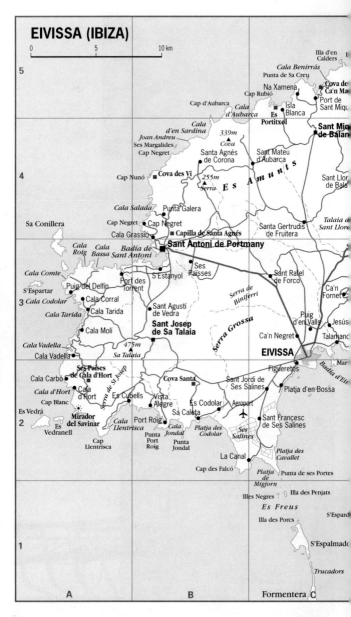

EIVISSA (IBIZA)

0   5   10 km

Illa d'en Calders
Cala Benirràs
Punta de Sa Creu
Cova de Ca'n Ma
Cap Rubió
Na Xamena
Port de Sant Miqu
Cap d'Aubarca
Cala d'Aubarca
Es Blanca
Isla
Portitxol
Sant Mic de Balan
Cala d'en Sardina
Joan Andreu
Ses Margalides
Cap Negret
339m
Cova
Santa Agnés de Corona
Sant Mateu d'Aubarca
Sant Llor de Bala
Cap Nunó
Cova des Vi
255m
Serra
Es Amunts
Cala Salada
Punta Galera
Santa Gertrudis de Fruitera
Talaia a Sant Llore
Sa Conillera
Cap Negret
Cap Negret
Cala Grassió
Capilla de Santa Agnés
Sant Antoni de Portmany
Cala Roig
Cala Bassa
Badia de Sant Antoni
Ses Païsses
Sant Rafel de Forco
Ca'n Fornet
Cala Comte
S'Estanyol
S'Espartar
Puig del Delfín
Port des Torrent
Serra de Biniferri
Cala Codolar
Cala Corral
Cala Tarida
Sant Agustí de Vedra
Puig d'en Valls
Jesús
Cala Tarida
Cala Tarida
Serra Grossa
Cala Molí
Sant Josep de Sa Talaia
Ca'n Negret
Talamanc
EIVISSA
Cala Vadella
475m
Sa Talaia
Figueretes
Mar
Badia d'Eiv
Ses Païsses de Cala d'Hort
Cova Santa
Sant Jordi de Ses Salines
Cala Carbó
Platja d'en Bossa
Cala d'Hort
Cala d'Hort
Cala Blanc
Es Cubells
Vista Alegre
Es Codolar
Aeroport
Ses Salines
Es Vedrà
Es Vedranell
Mirador del Savinar
Cala Llentrisca
Port Roig
Cala Jondal
Platja des Codolar
Sant Francesc de Ses Salines
Cap Llentrisca
Punta Port Roig
Punta Jondal
Sa Caleta
La Canal
Platja des Cavallet
Cap des Falcó
Platja de Migjorn
Punta de ses Portes
Illes Negres
Illa des Penjats
Es Freus
S'Espard
Illa des Porcs
S'Espalmado
Trucadors
A   B   Formentera   C

Cala
Portinatx
Punta
Moscarter
a
la
ac Portinatx
Cala de Serra
Port de Ses Caletes
Ses Caletes
Sant Vicenç
de sa Cala
Cova des
Culleram
Punta des Jonc
Clot des Llamp
Punta Grossa
Cala de Sant Vicenç
Cala de Sant Vicenç
Joan
britia
Serra de la Mala Costa
S'Aigua Blanca
Es Figueral
Platja des Figueral
409m
Es Fornás
Ximaina
Sant Carles
de Peralta
Museo es Trui
de Ca'n Andreu
Punta
d'en
Valls
Tagomago
Ca'n Jordi
Cap Roig
Cala Boix
La Joya
Cala Mastella
Cala Nova
Cala Llenya
S'Argamassa
Es Canar
218m
Puig d'en Ribes
Puig de
Missa
Punta Arabí
Cala
Pada
Punta Arabí
Santa Eulària des Riu
La Siesta
Cala Blanca
If Course
Cala Llonga
Roca Llisa
Cala Olivera

FORMENTERA

0   5 km

Illa des Porcs
S'Espardell
S'Espalmador
Port de
S'Espalmador
Trucadors
Ses Illetes
Platja de
Llevant
Punta de
Sa Pedrera
Cala
Savina
Ses Salines
La Savina
Estany
des Peix
Estany
Pudent
Ca-na
Costa
Platja des Pujols
Punta Prima
Punta de
Sa Gavina
Torre de
Sa Gavina
Es Pujols
Sant Francesc
de Formentera
Sant Ferran
VIA
Cuevas de
Xeroni
MAJOR
Platja de
Tramuntana
Punta
Palmera
Cala Saona
Punta
Rasa
Cala
Saona
Platja
Migjorn
Platja de Migjorn
Es Caló
El Pilar
de la Mola
Far de
la Mola
107m
192m
La Mola
Punta de Sa Ruda
Cala Codolar
Punta de
s'Anguila
Mar y Land
Punta de Sa
Fragata
Punta Roja
Torre des
Garroveret
Cap de Barbaria

D   E   F

Ibiza

There are several Ibizas, each distinctly different. At the island's heart, though not at its centre, is Eivissa, the capital. Even here there are several different towns – the old walled city of Dalt Vila and the Carthaginian necropolis beside it; the trendy shopping area near the harbour where visitors crowd to see the latest Ad Lib fashions; and the new town where more elegant shops and pavement cafés stand among the offices.

There are several coasts, too. Mass tourism has peopled some beaches with sun-worshippers and hotel developments have blighted the natural scenery. Yet within a few minutes' walk of these areas the visitor can be alone in coves as beautiful as any to be found on the Mediterranean coast.

Finally there is inland Ibiza, rural villages of white cube houses and black-shawled women, and upland areas where ancient vegetation still thrives. Here the plant lover can search for flowers found only on Ibiza, while the bird lover will delight in rare and exotic species.

'That whiteness: it exorcises all that is sordid.'

FAJARNES CARDONA
Ibizan poet

Eivissa

There are few more dramatic sites on the Mediterranean coast than that of Eivissa's Old Town, Dalt Vila, especially when viewed from the sea, its walls and bastions rising above the rugged coast and turquoise water.

Under Franco's centralist regime only Castillian names were allowed in areas of Spain that had their own language or dialect. Then, and still occasionally, the town was merely 'La Vila' to the locals, 'Ibiza Town' to visitors.

La Marina, Eivissa

However, democracy has allowed regional pride to flourish and many of the island's names are now both written and spoken in Ibizenco, a dialect of Catalan. In Ibizenco the town is Eivissa, a name that echoes the ancient names of the island – the Carthaginian *Ibosim*, the Greek *Ebysos*, the Roman *Ebusus* and the Moorish *Yebisah*.

Eivissa is a marvellous place in summer, an exciting assault on the senses. Within its close confines it captures the essence of the island – Dalt Vila, Sa Penya, La Marina and the local coast offering quite different aspects of Ibiza. Go to Dalt Vila for historical Ibiza, to Sa Penya's tight-knit streets for shopping and local colour, to La Marina or the harbour for the smell of the sea and to gape at the expensive boats, and to the nearby beaches for the modern, brasher Ibiza.

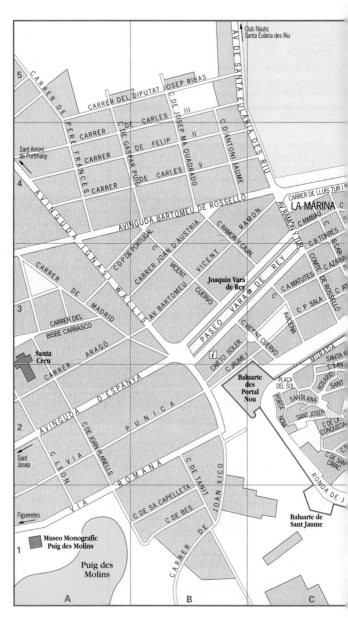

Club Nàutic
Santa Eulària des Riu

AV DE SANTA EULÀRIA DES RIU

CARRER DE PERE FRANCES

CARRER DEL DIPUTAT JOSEP RIBAS

C DE JOSEP Mª QUADRADO

C DE JOSEP III

CARRER DE CARLES III

C DE GASPAR PUIG

CARRER DE FELIP II

CARRER DE CARLES V

C D'ANTONI JAUME

Sant Antoni
de Portmany

AVINGUDA IGNASI WALLIS

AVINGUDA BARTOMEU DE ROSSELLÓ

LA MARINA

CARRER DE LLUÍS TUR I

C RIMBAU

C DP DE PORTUGAL

CARRER JOAN D'AUSTRIA

AV BARTOMEU

VICENT

VICENT

CUERVO

C RAMON Y CAJAL

RAMON

Joaquín Vara
de Rey

PASEO VARA DE REY

AV RAMON YUR

C B TORRES

COMTE DE ROSSELLÓ

C AZARIA

C BARGA

C A MATUTES

C P SALA

AVICENA

CARRER DE MADRID

CARRER DEL
BISBE CARRASCO

Santa
Creu

CARRER

DE

ARAGÓ

CANETO SOLER

C VICENT CUERVO

AVICENA

C JAUME I

Baluarte
des
Portal
Nou

MURADA

SANTA

C SAN

PLAÇA
DEL SOL

SANTA ANA

PORTA NOVA

SANT JOSEP

ROSARIO

SANT

C DE LA
CONQUISTA

C DE SAN
CIRIAC

C C

AVINGUDA D'ESPANYA

C DE JOAN PLANELLS

C LEON

C VIA

PUNICA

ROMANA

VIA

Sant
Josep

C DE SA CAPELLETA

C DE BES

C DE TANIT

CARRER DE JOAN XICO

RONDA DE J

Figueretes

Baluarte de
Sant Jaume

Museo Monografic
Puig des Molins

CARRER DE

Puig des
Molins

5

4

3

2

1

A

B

C

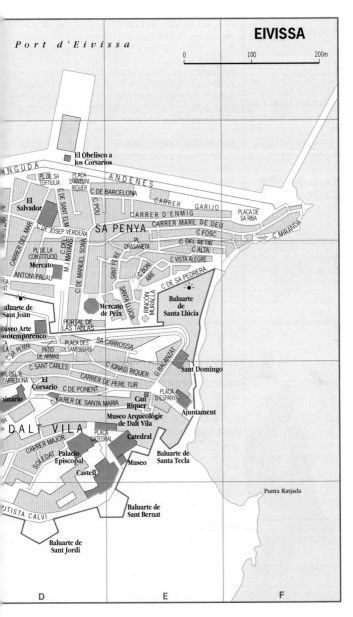

Port d'Eivissa

EIVISSA

0   100   200m

El Obelisco a
los Corsarios

NGUDA
PL DE SA
TERTULIA
PLAÇA
D'ANTONI
RIQUER
ANDENES
C DE BARCELONA
C DE SANT ELM
C POU
CARRER   GARIJO
PLAÇA DE
SA RIBA
El
Salvador
C DE JOSEP VERDERA
CARRER D'ENMIG
CARRER DEL MAR
SA PENYA
CARRER MARE DE DEU
C MIRANDA
PL DE LA
CONSTITUCIÓ
C DEL
M J MAYANS
C DE MANUEL SORA
PL
DRASANETA
SANT PERE
C FOSC
C ALTA
C DEL RETIR
C VISTA ALEGRE
Mercato
ANTONI PALAU
C BON
C AIRE
SANTA LLUCIA
C DE SA PEDRERA
SA
NT
aluarte de
Sant Joan
Mercato
de Peix
RINCÓN
MURALLA
Baluarte
de
Santa Llúcia
úseo Arte
ontemporenco
C SA PENYA
PORTAL DE
LAS TABLAS
SA CARROSSA
PLAÇA DES
DESAMPARATS
PL DEL R
ARREDONA
PATIO
DE ARMAS
C SANT CARLES
C IGNASI RIQUER
G BALANZAT
Sant Domingo
El
Corsario
CARRER DE PERE TUR
C DE PONENT
inario
CARRER DE SANTA MARIA
Can
Riquer
PLAÇA
D'ESPANYA
Ajuntament
Museo Arqueològic
de Dalt Vila
DALT VILA
CARRER MAJOR
PLAÇA
CATEDRAL
Catedral
SOLEDAT
Palacio
Episcopal
Castell
Museo
Baluarte de
Santa Tecla
UTISTA CALVI
Punta Ratjada
Baluarte de
Sant Bernat
Baluarte de
Sant Jordi

D   E   F

What to See in Eivissa

BALUARTE DE SANT BERNAT ●●

Between the cathedral (➤ 17) and the palace/castle (➤ below) a narrow alley leads to the Baluarte de Sant Bernat, from where there is a magnificent view. Straight ahead, and visible on most days, is Formentera, while to the right the southern part of Ibiza can be seen beyond the beaches of Figueretes and Platja d'en Bossa. Directly below is the rugged coast that forms the foreground for the wonderful view of the Dalt Vila (➤ 20) from the Formentera ferry.

33E1
Several choices near by (£–£££)
Not on a bus route
None
Free access

BALUARTE DE SANTA LLÚCIA ●●

Those following the line of the old walls – a circuit is a little under 2km and worth the effort – will eventually reach the triangular bastion of Baluarte de Santa Llúcia, its long sides aligned with the harbour and the coast to give maximum range to its artillery. From the bastion there is a splendid view over the huddle of houses and narrow alleys of Sa Penya (➤ 38) to La Marina (➤ 35) and Eivissa's harbour.

33E3
Several choices near by (£–£££)
Not on a bus route
None
Free access

CASTLE AND EPISCOPAL PALACE ●

The Castle (Castell) and Episcopal Palace (Palacio Episcopal) stand across from the cathedral (➤ 17) and Archaeological Museum (➤ 36), though they are at present inaccessible due to their ruinous state. The castle dates from at least the time of the Moors and is almost certainly older. Sadly, the numerous rebuildings, necessary both to modify the defences in line with changes in weaponry and to satisfy the desires of the latest island ruler, created an odd assortment of bits and pieces which required continuous upkeep. When the need for a fortress declined in the 19th century, maintenance stopped and the castle fell into disrepair. Today only a section of the keep remains, as a picturesque ruin.

Opposite the castle stands the equally ruinous bishop's palace. In the mid-18th century Eivissa was given city status and became the seat of a bishop, though the palace predates that event by several centuries, having been built in the fine Gothic style of the first cathedral. At present both buildings are under repair, though the damage is so extensive that this is likely to be a very long-term venture. The visitor can see only one aspect of the restoration so far, the modern steps which rise across the alley from the cathedral.

33D2
Plaça Catedral, Dalt Vila
The Plaza del Sol (££), in the Plaça del Sol close to the Baluarte des Portal Nou
Closed for restoration
Not on a bus route
None

CATEDRAL (➤ 17, TOP TEN)

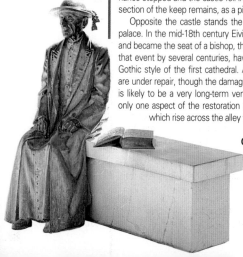

The statue of Isidor Macabich in Plaça des Desamparats

CHURCH OF SANT DOMINGO ⊙

Positioned between the Baluarte de Santa Lucia and Plaça d'Espanya, Sant Domingo is immediately recognisable by its delightful red-tiled cupolas. Inside there are 19th-century frescos, restored after a disastrous fire all but destroyed them.

✚	33E2
✉	Between Baluarte de Santa Lucia and Plaça d'Espanya
🍽	Several choices (£–£££)
🚌	Not on a bus route
♿	None Free access

DALT VILA (► 20, TOP TEN)

LA MARINA ⊙⊙

Though this is really a part of old Eivissa and therefore just an extension of Sa Penya (► 38), there is a world of difference between the rundown streets and houses of Penya and the up-market boutiques of fashionable La Marina. The difference, of course, is money – that of the entrepreneurs who have renovated the area and opened the shops, the cafés and the terrace bars, and that of the visitors who throng the narrow streets. But great though La Marina is for shopping – it is probably the best place on the island for just about everything – it is even better for people-watching. It seems that for many visitors to La Marina it is better to be seen than to see: the exotic eye-catching outfits of the shoppers or strollers offer free entertainment to anyone with the price of a coffee and an hour to spare.

La Marina is very compact – from the seafront cafés to the walls of Dalt Vila or the market square is less than 200m – so all of it can be examined in detail in a couple of hours, but if you are really pressed for time head for the four short, parallel streets of Rimbau, Bisbe Torres, Azaria and Arubal to find the best the area has to offer.

✚	32C4
🍽	Several choices (£–£££)
♿	Few

Above: *the red-tiled cupolas of Sant Domingo below the cathedral*

The newer, but just as attractive, section of Eivissa

🔢 33E2
✉️ 3 Plaça Catedral, Dalt Vila
☎️ 30 12 31
🕐 Apr–Sep Tue–Sat 10–2, 5–8, Sun 10–2; Oct–Mar Tue–Sat 10–1, 4–6, Sun 10–2
🍴 The Plaza del Sol (££), in the Plaça del Sol
🚌 Not on a bus route
♿ None
✋ Moderate
↔️ Cathedral Museum (► 17)

🔢 33D3
✉️ Ronda Narcis Puget, Dalt Vila
☎️ 30 27 23
🕐 Apr–Sep Mon–Fri 10–1:30, 5–8, Sat am
🍴 See above
🚌 Not on a bus route
♿ None ✋ Cheap

🔢 32B3
🍴 Several choices (£–£££)
♿ Few; accessible

MUSEO ARQUEOLÒGIE DE DALT VILA ✪✪✪

The Archaeological Museum is a small but excellent museum of the history of Ibiza and Formentera. It is so compact – though it does have a lot of steps – that a visit need only take an hour or so, but it will be a worthwhile hour, visitors gaining a useful insight into the lives of the Carthaginian, Roman and Moorish occupants of the islands. The museum's Carthaginian remains are particularly good: together with those from the Puig des Molins Museum (► 38) they represent the world's finest collection of artefacts from that most enigmatic of civilisations. All the displays within the museum have explanations in English as well as Spanish and Catalan.

MUSEO ARTE CONTEMPORENCO ✪

Situated in a fine old building that forms part of the Baluarte de San Juan, above the Plaça de Vila, the Museum of Contemporary Art specialises in the work of present-day painters, with work by Ibizan, other Spanish and some foreign artists. The museum is also the setting for numerous exhibitions of work by single artists or particular groups. Details can be found at the museum, the Tourist Information Office, or in the local newspapers.

NEW TOWN ✪

Close to La Marina is the newest part of Eivissa. Head for the Paseo Vara de Rey in the centre of which stands the monument to one of Ibiza's most famous sons. Here, too, are the Tourist Information Office and, opposite, Eivissa's best bookshop, which also sells foreign-language newspapers. The wide, elegant Paseo is well named, the Ibizencos, particularly the young, coming here for the evening's *paseo*.

An old Roman statue guards the Portal de las Tablas

PLAÇA D'ESPANYA ✪

At the extreme eastern edge of the Dalt Vila lies Plaça d'Espanya, another of the famous landmarks of the old town. Within there is a reclining statue of Guillem de Montgri, who captured the island in 1235.

The Ajuntament (Town Hall), which opens on to the square, occupies part of a large white building erected in the 17th century as a monastery for Dominican priests. Of the monastery, only the church (Sant Domingo, ➤ 35) remains.

From Plaça d'Espanya two excellent old streets head off westwards. Calle de Pere Tur has several fine mansions, one of which, Casa Riquer, was built by Antonio Riquer, among Ibiza's most famous – and, from the fine style of the house, most successful – pirates. Calle Major has an array of equally fine houses.

PORTAL DE LAS TABLAS ✪✪

Close to the market square (Plaça de la Constitució) of Sa Penya, the oldest section of the town outside the old walls, is the most imposing of the gates into the old town. Its name dates from medieval times, when there was a moat outside the gateway, the drawbridge across it being made of *tablas* (stone slabs). The inscription above the gate notes that Felipe (Philip) II was responsible for its construction in 1585. The portal is decorated with the king's coat-of-arms and a pair of Roman portal statues unearthed during the construction work. The inscription on one of the statues suggests it was originally raised to the goddess Juno.

Passing through the gateway (note the thickness of the wall: Charles V ordered that they be 2m thick) you will reach the Patio de Armas, the arsenal square. This beautifully colonnaded square has recently been restored, as has the archway that connects it to the equally delightful Plaça de Vila. The restoration work is excellent and the squares are a delight, but there are those who fear that the beautifying of the old town and the exodus of local folk who cannot afford the increased house prices will eventually mean a loss of character for Dalt Vila.

🍴 None in the square, but several near by (£–£££)
♿ Few; accessible

✚ 33D3
🍴 Several choices near by (£–£££)

37

✝ 32A1
✉ 31 Via Romana, Eivissa
☎ 30 17 31
🕐 Museum closed for
restoration, necropolis
remains open Apr–Sep
Tue–Sat 10–2 & 5–8, Sun
10–2; Oct–Mar Tue–Sat
10–1 & 4–6, Sun 10–2.
When museum re-opens
times will be as for
necropolis
🍴 The Plaza del Sol (££), in
the Plaça del Sol close to
the Baluarte des Portal
Nou
🚌 Not on a bus route
♿ None
👆 Moderate

✝ 33E4
🍴 Several choices (£–££)
♿ Few; accessible
🚌 Not on a bus route

The site of the
Carthaginian necropolis of
Puig des Molins

PUIG DES MOLINS   ❀❀❀

Beside Dalt Vila stands Puig des Molins, the Hill of
Windmills. Long before the windmills appeared (which are,
in any case, long gone), the hill was the largest necropolis of
Carthaginian Ibiza. Several thousand tombs have already
been found and excavated, and more almost certainly lie
below the olive groves and flower-covered slopes. Many of
the excavated finds from the necropolis, and from that at Es
Cuieram at the northeastern tip of the island, are exhibited in
the Museo Monografic Puig des Molins in Via Romana on
the town side of the hill. Outside the museum there is a
marked walkway through the necropolis.

One excavated site can be visited. It is known as the
Mule Hypogea because it was found when a mule fell
down the old tomb in 1946. Hypogea is the name given to
the Carthaginian method of interring the dead, one
excavation containing a number of side chambers in which
sarcophagi or cremated remains were placed.

SA PENYA   ❀

At the far end of the harbour from Eivissa's new town,
crammed into the narrow strip of land between Dalt Vila
and the sea, is Sa Penya, the oldest section of the town to
lie outside the medieval walls. How you view Sa Penya
depends upon your spirit of adventure. Some will see it as
the most interesting part of town, the place where the real
Ibizencos live. But for others its dark, narrow alleys will
seem forbidding, a good deal less salubrious than the
bright lights of the island's main tourist trap.

Traditionally, Sa Penya was the fishermen's quarter of
Eivissa and although it remains so for many who still earn a
living from the sea, it is now largely the preserve of the
island's poorest inhabitants. A tour is often interrupted by
lines of drying washing, fast-moving children or dogs, the
latter either frightened or frightening. Your nose will work
overtime deciphering odd cooking smells and your ears will
be bombarded by shouts and strange hammerings. Yet
there is an excitement and reality about Sa Penya that is
sometimes absent from the glossier shopping streets just
a stone's throw away.

To experience Sa Penya at its best, follow Carrer
d'enmig (the aptly named street in the middle) from Plaza
d'Antoni Riquer (go up Calle Pou and then turn second left)
to Plaça de Sa Riba at the harbour's end. Running parallel,
one street further from the sea, is Calle de la Virgen (called
Carrer Mare de Deu – Mother of God Street – in Catalan),
where some of the oldest houses in Eivissa are still
standing.

A Walk Around Eivissa

This walk starts by the sea.

Cross into Plaça d'Antoni Riquer and bear right to Plaça de Sa Tertiúlia. Turn sharp left (look for the San Telmo restaurant sign). At the T-junction turn left, then first right, to pass the new market.

The new market in Plaça de la Constitucio replaces the medieval one.

Go up the ramp through Portal de las Tablas (➤ 37) to reach the Plaça de Vila. Turn sharp left to the edge of Plaça des Desamparats, then left again. The Museum of Contemporary Art (➤ 36) is ahead: turn right along the old wall.

The seated figure in Plaça des Desamparats (below, right) is Isidor Macabich, priest and historian of Ibiza and Formentera.

Follow the wall to Baluarte de Santa Lúcia (➤ 34). Turn right towards the Church of Sant Domingo (➤ 35). Go up steps into Plaça d'Espanya. Bear right through the square and go straight along Carrer de Pere Tur. Turn left up steps and continue past the El Corsario Hotel. Go sharp left up steps to reach a T-junction. Turn right, going under an arch to reach a T-junction. Turn left to reach Plaça Catedral .

Here are the cathedral itself (➤ 17), the Archaeological Museum (➤ 36) and the Episcopal Palace/Castle (➤ 34).

Return down Carrer Major, bearing right along Carrer de Sant Ciriac, then right again. Go left down steps beside the Seminario.

The old Seminario is being converted into apartments.

Bear right to continue down the steps of Calle de la Conquista. Go straight on to a T-junction and turn right to reach Plaça del Regente Gotarredona. Fork left, then turn left down steps to return to the Plaça de Vila. Reverse the outward route back to the harbour.

Distance
2km

Time
2–4 hours, depending on the museums visited

Start/end point
The Corsairs Monument, near the harbour.
✚ 33D4

Lunch
Plaza del Sol (££)
✉ Plaça del Sol, close to the Baluarte des Portal Nou
☎ 39 07 73

Platja d'en Bossa – not a beach for those looking for solitude

The Beaches of Ibiza

This list of Ibiza's most popular beaches starts with those close to Eivissa and then moves clockwise around the island. 'Facilities' means the availability of food and drink, and the hire of sunbeds and watersport equipment. Note that there are no lifeguards on Ibizan beaches.

TALAMANCA 🔢 28C3
Lying just to the east of Eivissa. There are ferries from Eivissa's harbour at regular intervals during the day. Once regarded as shabby and even unclean, Talamanca has been cleaned up of late and though small is now perfectly acceptable. Excellent facilities.

SES FIGUERETES 🔢 28C2
On the other side of Eivissa from Talamanca. The beach is long but not too well kept. The promenade is its best feature. Good facilities.

PLATJA D'EN BOSSA 🔢 28C2
A continuation of Ses Figueretes and huge, almost 3km long. This is a package-holiday resort and so tends to be crowded, but with its palm trees, is very attractive. Excellent facilities.

PLATJA DES CAVALLET 🔢 28C2
This is Ibiza's official nudist beach and is less crowded than the other Eivissa beaches. Excellent facilities.

PLATJA DE MIGJORN (LAS SALINAS) 🔢 28C2
On the opposite side of Punta de ses Portes from Platja des Cavallet. Popular for its *chiringuitos*, but less so for its rocks. Excellent facilities.

PLATJA DES CODOLAR 🔢 28B2
Small and situated at the end of the airport runway, but with the compensation of magnificent views. Too stony for good sunbathing or swimming, but quiet. Poor facilities.

CALA JONDAL 🔢 28B2
Sand at the sea edge and pebbles further back, beneath beautiful, if unstable, cliffs. Good facilities.

CALA D'HORT (➤ 18, TOP TEN)

CALA VADELLA 🔢 28A3
A small beach in a cove popular with sailors. Excellent facilities. See also ➤ 49.

CALA TARIDA ✚ 28A3
A long sandy beach ideal for children. Excellent facilities.

SANT ANTONI ✚ 28B3
There are several beaches close to Sant Antoni. Cala Comte is small but has reasonable facilities. Cala Bassa is much larger and has excellent facilities. Port des Torrent is small but has excellent facilities. Cala Grassió, to the north of the town, is very small and surprisingly quiet, but facilities are limited. Cala Salada, the next beach northwards, is larger and offers good swimming, but has limited facilities.

CALA BENIRRÁS ✚ 28C5
Close to Port de Sant Miguel and very popular with the locals. Sand and rocks. Limited facilities.

CALA XARRACA ✚ 29D5
Small, with limited facilities, but very beautiful. See also ➤ 49.

PORTINATX ✚ 29D5
There are several beaches here, all with excellent facilities. See also ➤ 61.

CALA DE SANT VICENÇ ✚ 29E5
A beautiful cove with excellent facilities.

PLATJA DES FIGUERAL ✚ 29E4
The northern end of Figueral (Agua Blanca) is difficult to reach and usually very quiet, but has very limited facilities. The long southern end has good facilities.

CALA BOIX ✚ 29E4
Just to the north of Cala Mastella, this very pretty cove has curiously coloured greenish sand but is excellent for swimming. Reasonable facilities.

CALA MASTELLA ✚ 29E4
A marvellous little cove with excellent swimming, but limited facilities. See ➤ 46.

ES CANAR/SANTA EULÀRIA/CALA LLONGA ✚ 29D3
These are package-holiday centres, which unfortunately means crowds, but they have excellent facilities.

Aquamar, on Platja d'en Bossa, one of the beach's many facilities

What to See in Ibiza

BALAFIA ●●●

Visitors with a sense of adventure can approach the village
(► 16) from the Church of Sant Llorenç. This delightful
building is curiously unstructured, due to its being originally
built in the late 18th century, but with sections added over
the following 60 years or so.

Take the lane on the left side of the church. The first
building passed is Can Pere Mosson, with a tall medieval
refuge tower. There is a spring here, and also an old
Roman olive press which is now used as a watertrough.
Continue along the rough, narrow lane to reach Balafia.
One of the interesting features about both Can Pere
Mosson and Balafia is that the towers and buildings are
sometimes only part-whitewashed and have a white cross
on the exposed brick or stonework. These crosses were to
ward off evil spirits.

CALA D'HORT ●●●

Cala d'Hort is rightly one of the most popular spots on Ibiza
(► 18), its main drawback being a lack of parking for those
with their own transport. Come early, or try the parking
areas at the cliff top before the road descends to the bay.
The walk from here is longer, but the views are
outstanding.

Close to Cala d'Hort – take the road for Cala Vadella – is
Ses Païses de Cala d'Hort, the excavated ruin of a country
house dating from the late Carthaginian/early Roman
period of Ibiza's history. The site, signposted from the road
and reached by a rough track which must be walked,
includes the remains of walls and a small Punic necropolis.

+ 29D4
⊠ Close to the
Eivissa–Portinatx road
🍴 Ca-na Pepeta (£), on the
main road
🚌 Eivissa–Portinatx
♿ None
🎫 Free

+ 28A2
⊠ At the southwestern tip
of the island
🍴 The Cala d'Hort (£), at the
beach or the Es Boldado
(££), reached by a stiff
walk or by a rough track
from the Cala Vadella
road
🚌 Not on a bus route, but
many resorts organise
coach travel
♿ Few
🎫 Free

*A perfect place for lunch,
the beach restaurant at
Cala d'Hort*

CALA LLONGA ⭐

Before the advent of mass tourism, Cala Llonga was one of the scenic highlights of the island. The bay is long and narrow (by Ibizan standards), more like a Norwegian fjord in miniature than the characteristic half-moon shape of Ibiza. At one time, rocks topped with typical coastal scrub blazed white in the sun on either side of the fjord which ended with a 200m beach of white sand.

Then the developers came, building hotels and apartments. How visitors react to such development depends upon their standpoint. The hotels and apartments have brought wealth and prosperity to the island and the local economy, and bring pleasure into the lives of countless holidaymakers. But at the same time they have not added to the scenic delights of this most delightful of bays.

On the positive side, Cala Llonga's sheltered beach is one of the best on the island for children and it is still possible to enjoy Cala Llonga's scenery: take the coastal path that leaves the centre of the 'village' of Cala Llonga, going uphill to Puig Marina. The path requires perseverance but soon, beyond the hilltop, a small valley is reached. To the right here a tunnel (it is quite short so no torch is required) leads to Cala Blanca, a bay without a beach. Swimming is possible from the rocks. To return, stay closer to the cliff edge, rounding Punta Roja for a view along Cala Llonga's fjord.

🕂 29D3
✉ On the coast between Eivissa and Santa Eulària
🍴 Range of restaurants (£–£££)
🚌 Reached by buses from either town
♿ Reasonable

Cala Llonga: many feel this lovely cove has been spoilt by tourism and development

Did you know ?

Those seeking alternative relaxation can head south of Cala Llonga to reach Roca Llisa and Ibiza's only golf course, originally built as 9-hole course. More recently a full 18-hole course has been opened, giving 27 holes in all.

In the Know

If you only have a short time to visit Ibiza or Formentera, or would like to get a real flavour of the islands, here are some ideas:

10
Ways To Be A Local

Buy an easel and paints and set up as a pavement artist in a square in Dalt Vila.

Get a fishing rod and stand above the sea for hours, catching nothing.

Learn to use a *porrón* (➤ 99).

Learn to love paella. With all that sea out there the locals love fish in all its forms.

Relax – take a siesta. The noonday sun really is too hot to walk about in.

Learn to accept life's oddities – eg other tourists – with a smile or a shake of the head.

Take an evening stroll. Doing the *paseo* is an essential pastime.

Take an early-morning coffee at a pavement café and have an animated conversation with your companions, and take time out to watch the world go by.

Buy a small dog and a long lead: everybody in town has one.

Borrow a small car or, if you are young, a scooter.

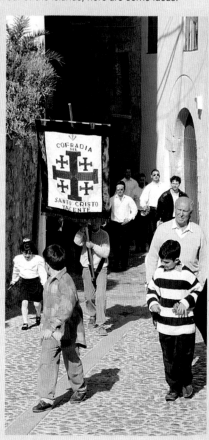

An Easter Sunday procession to Dalt Vila's cathedral: scenes like this can be found all over the island

10
Good Places To Have Lunch

Cala Boix (£) Cala Boix ☎ 33 52 24 . Excellent menu near a remote cove.

Cas Mallorqui (££)
✉ At the road's end in Portinatx ☎ 33 30 82. Fish only, but some of the best on the island, and a wonderful view.

Casa Rafael (£)
✉ Carrer d'Isidor Macabich, Sant Françesc, Formentera. Where the locals eat – what more is there to say?

Es Pla (££) ✉ Beside the road to Cala Saona, just after the turn from the main road, Formentera ☎ 32 27 09. Classic Formentera cooking.

Hacienda Na Xamena (£££) ✉ Near Port de Sant Miquel ☎ 33 45 00. The dearest buffet lunch on Ibiza, but memorable.

Insulata Augusta (££) ✉ At far end of Platja d'en Bossa ☎ 39 08 82. With a terrace on the beach.

Pizzeria Magu (£) ✉ At harbour end of the seafront, Santa Eulària ☎ 33 93 26. The best pizza for miles (and good meat and pasta too), and a view of the seafront.

Plaza del Sol (££) ✉ Plaça del Sol, Dalt Vila ☎ 39 07 73. Close to one of Dalt Vila's *baluartes*, with a classic view.

Ruta (££) ✉ 44–48 Plaça de la Iglesia, Sant Josep ☎ 80 05 44. Good plain cooking in delightful surroundings.

Tio Bigotis Chiringuito (£) ✉ Cala Mastella. Romantic setting and equally romantic host.

10
Top Activities

- Bird-watching
- Cycling
- Diving or snorkelling
- Going to a *ball páge*
- Sailing
- Sunbathing
- Taking a boat ride
- Tennis
- Walking
- Water-skiing

10
Souvenir Ideas

- Ad Lib fashions
- Embroidery
- *Hierbas* (the typical herbal liqueur of the islands)
- Jewellery
- Knitwear from Formentera
- Leatherware
- Traditional musical instruments from Formentera
- Paintings
- Pottery
- Wickerwork

2
Official Nude Beaches

- Es Cavallet on Ibiza
- Ses Illetes on Formentera

5
'Unofficial Official' Nude Beaches

- S'Aigua Blanca
- Cala Olivera
- Las Salinas (the rocky, eastern end)
- Platja de Llevant on Formentera
- Platja de Tramuntana on Formentera

5
Good Beaches For Children

- Platja de Talamanca
- Cala Tarida
- Cala Llonga
- Es Canar
- Platja de Migjorn on Formentera

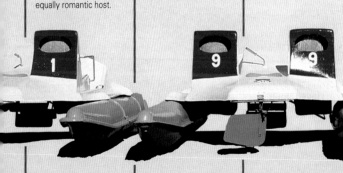

🔲 29E4

✉️ From the centre of Sant
Carles, take the road
signposted for Cala
Llenya and Cala Mastella.
In the village of La Joya,
turn left. Just before Cala
Llenya is reached a road
on the left is signed for
Cala Mastella. To reach
the (limited) parking, go
past the Sa Seni
restaurant and take the
steep, rough track on the
left

🍴 Two restaurants,
including Tio Bigotis
Chiringuito (£)

🚌 Not on a bus route

♿ None; access difficult

*Cala Mastella, not easy to
get to but all the more
appealing as a result*

CALA MASTELLA ⭐⭐

There is a beach at Cala Mastella, but it is small – only 50m
long and 10m wide – so most swimmers use the rocks at
the bay's edges, or the wall of the tiny port, as their
platform. The waters here are clear and clean, the whole
bay a delight, not least because development has been
kept to a minimum and the relatively difficult access keeps
visitor numbers within manageable limits.

Most of those who came will be heading for the bay's
open-air café/bar, the Tio Bigotis Chiringuito – follow the
well-worn path across the rocks on the bay's left side. The
curious name derives from the *bigotis* – moustache – of
the owner, Jóan Ferrer. Señor Ferrer's boat is moored in
Mastella's little port as he is a fisherman as well as a cook.
Some days the café is so full that you may not be able to
get a table before the day's stock of fish has been eaten.
Be philosophical – book your table for another day and go
for a swim or explore the rocks at the bay's edge. When
the day of your booking arrives, be sure to arrive early –
just in case. Then, when you do sit down, try the *bullit de
peix*, an incomparable fish stew.

Close to Cala Mastella is another fine bay, Cala Boix
(► 41). This is also signposted, and from its car park steps
descend to a good beach. Here, too, there are bar/restau-
rants which, though excellent, do not have the romantic
appeal of the Moustache.

The Ruta de Falcó Walk

Much of Ibiza's coast has been marked by the red-topped posts of the Route of the Falcon, a walk which explores the best of the island's coastline.

From the car park at Cala Boix, walk away from the sea to reach the track marked with the red-topped posts. Turn right beside the ruinous wall: do not take the track to Cap Roig. After a few minutes leave the posts by following a path on the right-hand side of a wall, ascending through almond groves to reach a wood. Follow the wall through the wood, but when it bears left continue ahead along an overgrown path, following it uphill, then down to a track. Turn left to a gate. Go through and turn right, following a track to the now obvious Torre d'en Valls.

Torre d'en Valls, a landmark on the walk

This is one of a series of watchtowers around the Ibizan coast which warned the islanders of pirate attacks. Offshore is the island of Tagomago (➤ 51).

Return along the track, but ignore your outward route to continue to reach the sea at Canal d'en Martí.

The bay is very remote and usually empty. Those wanting to make a day of the walk could have a swim and eat at the Salvado restaurant before continuing.

Follow the red-topped posts, then bear left along a farm track, walking with a wall on your left and a fig grove on your right. When the track bears left, continue along a path between walls. Descend to a streambed, then continue, soon reaching the point on the outward route where you turned right. Now follow the outward route back to Cala Boix.

Distance
6km

Time
3 hours

Start/end point
Cala Boix
➕ 29E4

Lunch
Cala Boix (£)
✉ Cala Boix
☎ 33 52 24
or
Salvado
✉ Pou des Lleo/Canal d'en Martí

A Drive Around Northeast Ibiza

Distance
65km

Time
6 hours

Start/end point
Eivissa
✚ 28C3

Lunch
Platja Sant Vicenç (£)
✉ Cala de Sant Vicenç

This drive follows Ibiza's western coast before turning inland through wonderful scenery to reach the main island road.

From Eivissa take the main road (the E10) signposted Santa Eulària, Portinatx, then bear right along the road signposted Jesús. Continue through the village (➤ 21) and, after 5km, pass the golf course. After a further 4km, bear left at the turn to Cala Llonga (➤ 43).

Go through Santa Eulària (➤ 26), following the road signposted Sant Carles, ignoring the right fork for Es Canar. After 8km, in Sant Carles (San Carlos), turn left at the T-junction, following the road signposted Cala de Sant Vicenç. After about 6km, as you near Sant Vicenç (San Vicent), the sign of a camera at the roadside indicates a good viewpoint (although there is no parking place other than the road itself, which can be a dangerous place to linger). The road reaches a T-junction.

Turn right here for a short detour and lunch at the beachside Platja Sant Vicenç.

The route turns to the left, signposted Sant Joan, Portinatx. After 3km, turn right along a narrow road which is signposted Sant Vicenç. Bear left past the church and follow a single-track road, bearing left by the sports court to rejoin the main road at a T-junction. Turn right.

After 6km you reach Sant Joan de Labritja (San Juan). Continue through the town and, after a further 2km, take the road that is signposted Eivissa. Follow the main road for 15km, passing Balafia (➤ 16) on the right, to reach a roundabout. Go straight across, signposted Eivissa, following the main road for a further 8km to reach a roundabout on the outskirts of Eivissa.

CALA VADELLA ★★

Many believed Vadella was Ibiza's most beautiful cove before the coming of mass tourism, though much of the tourist development is in the form of elegant, and expensive, villas discreetly hidden among the pines that back the beach. With its sheltering headlands, extremely fine-grained sand and amazingly clear water, Cala Vadella is excellent for swimming and there are good facilities, both at the beach and in the small village. Watersports equipment can be hired and the bars and restaurants are especially good. The cove is a fine natural harbour and there are ample opportunities for boat trips – some going as far as Formentera.

✚ 28A3
✉ North of Cala d'Hort, reached by a road from Cala d'Hort or from Sant Josep
🍴 Several choices (£–£££)
♿ Few; accessible

CALA XARRACA ★★★

Strictly speaking, Cala Xarraca is a tiny half-moon bay cut into the inner arc of a much larger cove, one enclosed by the headlands of Punta sa Torre near Portinatx, and Xarraca to the west. On the Portinatx side of the bay a path heads easily around a shallow headland to a much smaller bay. Follow this path to reach Cala Xuela, a little more crowded because of the closeness of the main road, but still very attractive.

✚ 29D5
✉ Beside a sharp bend of the C733
🍴 Cala Xarraca (£), beach
🚌 Eivissa–Portinatx
♿ None

Heading away from Portinatx you can pick up a path at the far end of the beach: follow this to a picturesque small bay with boathouses and curiously painted rocks. Bear right to continue through the pines to reach clumps of almond, fig and olive trees. Now turn right to reach a marvellous viewpoint back towards Portinatx. On the main path you will pass a *finca* (old farmhouse). Soon afterwards, a right turning leads to the Xarraca headland, from where the views are outstanding. From the end of the path, which is about a half-hour's walk from the beach at Cala Xarraca, steps lead down to the sea.

Cala Vadella, one of Ibiza's most sheltered bays

Many stories have grown up around Cova Santa, a small cave near Sa Caleta

COVA SANTA ⚫

Cova Santa means Holy Cave, though the name is the subject of conflicting legends. One story has it that in medieval times, perhaps even earlier, a Christian hermit lived in the cave. An alternative tale is that the waters of the cave had healing properties and were much sought after in medieval times. It is known to have been used as a refuge by local folk during times of danger as long ago as the 15th century.

The cave is about 25m deep and has some excellent stalagmites and stalactites, but getting to see them can be a problem: there seem to be no fixed opening times, and there is no telephone. A small shop sells souvenirs, chiefly local *hierbas* (➤ 57).

ES CANAR ⚫

Es Canar (Es Caná) is a lively modern resort town aimed at families. As a link with its past, there is a tiny harbour where tiny fishing boats are moored while their owners dry or mend nets.

The town lies on the northern side of the headland of Punta Arabí (➤ 62) and a fine two-hour walk from Es Canar follows the coast around Punta Arabí and on into Santa Eulària. There are boats linking the two towns for a more relaxing return trip.

The beach of Es Canar is a graceful curve, its sands covered with sunbeds and parasols, and the waters of the bay are completely current-free, making it one of *the* safest – many say *the* safest – on Ibiza for children. It is possible to hire all kinds of watersports equipment here, or to join a boat trip that will help you to explore the local coast from a different perspective.

ES CUBELLS

The road to Es Cubells from Sant Josep passes through fine country planted at intervals with olives and vines. It is an attractive little village studded with stands of pine trees and has a collection of luxurious island homes perched above the coast.

Within the village an old monastery has been converted to a school, while a theological college stands high on a rocky outcrop. To complete this scene of piety there is a fine village church.

From Es Cubells a road runs high above the cliffs towards the headland of Cap Llentrisca. Also worth visiting if you have the time is the more modern village of Vista Alegre, reached by taking the other branch at the road fork close to Es Cubells.

28A2

From Sant Josep a road heads due south; continue past the turning to Vista Allegre

A few good restaurants

The village is not on a bus route

Reasonable, but difficult to reach without a car

ES FIGUERAL

Es Figueral is divided into two: the roads reaching the beaches of Figueral and S'Aigua Blanca are separated by a few hundred metres of undrivable sand and cliffs. A third road leads to the cliff-top German Garten café.

Agua Blanca lies to the north, its name reflecting the fact that the water is white as it laps the shore due to the strong and frequent winds that blow across the open bay. The beach itself has a darker sand than the island norm and has become popular with nudists. Facilities are few, but there is a good bar.

To the south of Es Figueral, off the headland of Punta d'en Valls, is Illa de Tagomago. There are frequent boat trips to this uninhabited island which has retained its wild character. The beaches are too small for serious sunbathing, but the swimming is superb and the scuba diving excellent.

29D4

Between Punta Grossa to the north and Punta d'en Valls to the south

Club Cala Blanca (££); Garten café (£)

From Santa Eulàlia

Reasonable

Looking towards the Illa de Tagomago from the cliffs above Es Figueral

ISLA BLANCA ●●

28C5

From Sant Mateu, take the road towards Sant Miquel. At a T-junction turn left along the road signed for Es Portitxol

There are no buses to the area

None

As the coast is neared, the road to Isla Blanca drops steeply and becomes rough. On reaching a low-roofed ruin the road drops again to the right to reach the sea. The track to the left becomes blocked after a short while, continuing as a rough path below ominous slabs of rock that have fallen from the vertical cliffs.

This is a wonderful section of coast, quiet and secret, and with stunning views. There is no beach for sunbathing, but the swimming is excellent, the water so clear that from the cliff top you can watch the progress of cormorants as they swim underwater in pursuit of fish.

JESÚS ●●●

28C3

Just off the Eivissa–Cala Llonga road

Bon Lloc (££), on the main road through Jesús, close to the church

Eivissa–Santa Eulària

Good

Free

The road linking Eivissa to Cala Llonga and Santa Eulària runs through Jesús (► 21), occasionally turning the pretty little village, with its fine views of Dalt Vila, into a noisy place.

Close to the church there is always peace and quiet, however. Standing beside a small park with cacti and trees, it is reached via an elegant walkway with double lamps on wrought-iron posts. While strolling along the walkway, or admiring the trees in the park, it is easy to imagine how Ibiza must have felt when the donkey cart was the major form of island transport – though now and then the rattle of a passing lorry brings you back to reality.

The beautiful northern coast of Ibiza near Isla Blanca

A Walk to Ibiza's Highest Point

As might be expected, there is a lot of climbing on this walk up to the island's highest point.

The walk starts from the church in Sant Josep (San José). From it, cross the road and walk up along the left-hand side of the bar (Carrer del Jordi).

There is a sign on the bar's wall indicating that this is the way to Sa Talaia.

At the T-junction at the top of the road – opposite the Destino, the best tapas bar for miles – turn right. Soon another sign points left along a rough track. Follow the track through terraced 'fields', soon reaching a pine wood.

The radio transmitters ahead are almost – but not quite – at the top of the hill.

Continue up the track, occasionally climbing steps cut into the rock, to reach the transmitters.

The climb to the transmitters takes about an hour, but is worthwhile for the view. As you take a well-earned rest and drink, look north across Badía de Sant Antoni (Sant Antonio Bay) and the west Ibizan coast, and then out across the beautiful country near Sant Josep.

To reach the actual high point, marked by further transmitters, follow the rough road southwards.

This section of the walk has only one advantage, however, that of reaching the highest point on the island, as the views from the top are limited by the total pine tree cover.

To return to Sant Josep, reverse the outward route.

Distance
6km (but a lot of climbing)

Time
3 hours

Start/end point
Sant Josep de sa Talaia
✚ 28B3

Lunch
Take a picnic, or try the Ruta (££) after finishing the walk
✉ 44–48 Plaça de la Iglesia, Sant Josep
☎ 80 05 44

Looking towards Sant Antoni from Sa Talaia's lower peak

➕ 28B2
✉ Take the Sant Josep road out of Eivissa, shortly bearing left towards the airport. Soon, bear left again towards Las Salinas and the beaches of Es Cavallet & Migjorn
🍴 Good choice (££)
🚌 There are regular buses from Eivissa
♿ Few

Above: *the canals and salt pans of Las Salinas*

LAS SALINAS ✪

Salt production is Ibiza's only true industry, and certainly the only one that is not connected to tourism. Ibizan salt is still highly prized, as it is very pure. The process is very simple: the salt pans are situated below sea level and at intervals the sluices are opened to allow water in and then the sluices are shut. For the next three months or so the sun does the hard work, evaporating the water to leave a crust of shimmering white salt on the pan's clay floor. The salt is then dug out of the pan and loaded on to ships for export.

The Carthaginians and other early trading nations needed salt to preserve their food during long sea voyages. Interestingly, one of the chief customers of Ibizan salt today is the Faroe Islands, where it is still used to salt fish: both the production process and the final uses are unchanged after 2,500 years. Today, Ibiza exports around 70,000 tons of salt annually.

Did you know ?

Salt was so important to medieval Ibiza that criminals were required to work on the salt pans throughout every day of their sentence.

Until 1715 each islander received a share in the profits of salt sales. After that date, when the Spanish government took over the salt business (and its profits), the islanders received a free ration of salt each year. This practice only ended a century ago when the government sold the industry to a private company.

MIRADOR DEL SAVINAR ●●

From the parking spot just off the Cala d'Hort road, continue along the track to reach a broad area of cliff top. To the left from here a steep and somewhat vague path climbs to the object of the walk – the old watchtower overlooking Isla Vedra. It is one of the best preserved on the coast. Follow the path with care; the combination of polished rocks and windblown sand – the latter acting like ball bearings – means the ascent is slippery.

Some maps of Ibiza show the tower marked as Torre des Savinar, others as Torre del Pirata. What is not in dispute, however, is its purpose, the tower having been constructed some time between the 16th and 18th centuries as a look-out for pirates approaching Ibiza's southern shore. The towers are known as *talaias* in Ibizenco, an interesting name as the island's highest peak is known as Sa Talaia. Presumably at one stage it, too, was used to watch for invaders.

The towers were constructed all around the island within sight of each other so that a beacon fire lit at one could rapidly pass a danger signal to all the islanders.

From the tower the eye is drawn to Isla Vedrá, home, legend has it, of the Sirens who lured sailors to their doom in Homer's story of Odysseus (Ulysses). The island is one of the most famous of all Ibizan landmarks, seen on hundreds of postcards. It is at its most picturesque when viewed from here, where its sheer cliffs are seen rising about the smaller island of Es Vendranell.

✚ 28A2

✉ Take the road for Cala d'Hort and turn along a track signed Torre des Savinar. Parking is possible on this track close to the road; further on the track becomes increasingly rough

🍴 None

🚌 Not on a bus route

♿ None; inaccessible

Es Vedranell and Es Vedrá from the Mirador del Savinar

Food & Drink

The cuisine of the Pine Islands reflects both their varied history and the impact of mass tourism on the islands. It is therefore possible to find a Carthaginian menu (though you have to look hard) along with fish and chips and a pint of beer – the latter served in an 'authentic' pub.

Paella
This is a Valencian dish named for the iron pan in which the rice is cooked. Remember that paella is only served at lunchtime and is always cooked to order, usually for a minimum of two people.

Pine Island Cuisine

Generally, Pine Island cuisine, as might by expected, is similar to that of mainland Spain, intermingled with dishes of its own. It is based chiefly on fish from the surrounding sea and chicken and game birds.

Gazpacho, an Andalusian soup thickened with bread and highly flavoured with peppers, onion and garlic, and served chilled, is very popular, as are *tortillas* (omelettes) and *paella*. Pine Island *Tortilla Española* (Spanish omelette), with potatoes and onions, tends to be more flan-like, while the Pine Island version of paella, *arroz* or *arrosec*, has meat (usually rabbit) and vegetables as well as fish and shellfish. In addition to *gazpacho*, the Pine Islands offer several good fish soups – try *bullit de peix*, or *sopa de rap* which is made with monkfish. *Guisat de peix* is a fish-based stew, while *guisat de marisc* is similar, but chiefly uses shellfish.

Fish Specialities

For a speciality fish dish, try *burrida de ratjada*, skate with a sauce that usually contains crushed toast and almonds. Often garlic is added to the sauce, though the fish's delicate flavour does mean that it survives very well without. *Tonyina al Eivissenca* is a particular Ibizan tuna dish, the fish being served in a sauce of pine nuts, eggs and white wine. Other worthwhile fish dishes are made with *salmonete* (red mullet), *mero* (grouper) and *mejillones* (mussels), while the local *langostinos* (langostines – Dublin Bay prawns) are excellent.

Bar Costa in Santa Gertrudis da Fruitera, one of the best-known bars on the island

Desserts

For dessert, try *ensaimada*, the typical Ibizan cake of a light pastry filled with cream or almond paste and sprinkled with sugar (*ensaimadas* are also served at breakfast), *orietas*, an aniseed cake, or *flaó*, a cheesecake flavoured with mint. *Flaó* is believed to be Carthaginian in origin.

Wines and Spirits

Spain produces very underrated wines, particularly from Rioja, but none of these come from the Pine Islands. Wine is made on the islands and can sometimes be found in restaurants (look for *vino de pàges*), but is more usually restricted to bars frequented by the locals. Island wine is red and is usually described as full-bodied. A reasonable translation of the description would be 'okay, but not worth a journey to find'.

Sangría is famous throughout Spain. As elsewhere, island *sangría* is a mixture of red wine, brandy, mineral water and fruit juice, served iced: depending on the mixture, it can have quite a kick.

The islands are famous for their herb spirits. *Hierbas* is herb-based – usually thyme, know locally as *frigola*, although other herbs are used occasionally – while *anis* is aniseed-based. Many of the local bars brew their own versions of these drinks, but be careful, the brews are usually very enticing and it is easy to forget how potent they are after a glass or two.

One of the joys of Ibiza is eating al fresco – whatever the time of day

Meat Dishes

Favourites include *safrit payes*, a filling stew of chicken and goat seasoned with garlic, and the Ibizan speciality of coles *a la Ibicenco*, a stew of pigs' ears and cabbage. On Formentera, pork is served with cinnamon and apples – a dish with a more general appeal. On both islands *sobrassades*, spicy sausages based on pork, are popular.

57

A Drive Around Southwest Ibiza

Distance
85km

Time
6 hours

Start/end point
Eivissa
✚ 28C3

Lunch
La Palmera
✉ Plaça de la Iglesia, Santa Inés

There are several roundabouts on the outskirts of Eivissa: follow signs for the airport and Sant Josep, finally reaching a point where the Sant Josep and airport roads diverge. Follow the road signposted for Sant Josep. After 9km, turn left at an awkward turning (on the crown of the bend) signposted Es Cubells. Follow the road for 4km to reach a T-junction. Turn left towards Es Cubells, then shortly turn right along a road signposted Cala d'Hort.

On reaching a T-junction, turn left to visit Cala d'Hort (➤ 18), a detour of about 5km. Otherwise, turn right towards Cala Vadella (➤ 49), following a section of road with excellent views over the west Ibizan coast. At the next T-junction, turn right towards Sant Josep (the left turn is to Cala Vadella). After 6km, at a T-junction with the main road, turn left towards Sant Antoni.

After 8km, at the roundabout with the oval sculpture on the outskirts of Sant Antoni, take the exit signposted Centro, Santa Agnés. Follow this road through beautiful country for 9km to reach a T-junction. To the left here there is a short detour to Santa Agnés (➤ 65) and the suggested lunch stop.

The route goes straight across along the road signposted Sant Mateu, Sant Miquel. Continue for 5km through almond groves and cultivated terraces to a T-junction. Turn right, signposted Santa Gertrudis, and follow the road into the village (➤ 70). Here, bear right along the main road signposted Eivissa. After 3km, go straight over at a roundabout until reaching the main C733 road. Bear right along the main road and follow it back to Eivissa.

Looking northwards from Sa Talaia

58

PORT DES TORRENT ⭐

This old village/port is now little more than an overflow of Sant Antoni de Portmany (► 66), though the small beach is pleasant and the rocks on its western edge offer a good walk.

A little to the west of Port des Torrent is Cala Bassa, a short bus ride from Sant Antoni. Although usually very busy, it is a beautiful bay with a beach over 200m long hemmed in by steep cliffs whose bases offer excellent snorkelling. For more peace, follow the obvious path from the road end, heading inland at first, but then curving with the bay to reach the cliff top at its western edge. From here there is a fine view towards San Antonio. The next bay is Cala Roig, on the western headland of which is a well-preserved watchtower. From the tower there is an impressive view across the sea to Sa Conillera. In Ibizan legend Conellera was the birthplace of Hannibal. There is a sheltered harbour and regular boats trips are made to it from Sant Antoni.

The island is excellent for lovers of flowers and lizards, but not good for swimmers, the large number of sea urchins creating misery for poorly placed feet. For that reason it is definitely not recommended for children, though snorkellers will have a very good time.

More easily reached from Port des Torrent is Cala Tarida. Here there is a long (300m) beach that is ideal for children. There are facilities for every conceivable water-sport and glass-bottomed boat trips are also available.

✚ 28A3
✉ On the western outskirts of Sant Antoni
🍴 Several choices (£–££)
🚌 Buses from Sant Antoni
♿ Reasonable

Above: *boat trips from Cala Bassa are popular*

59

 28C5

 The road from the C733 Eivissa–Portinatx road to Santa Gertrudis continues to Port de Sant Miquel

Cova de Ca'n Marça

The road from the C733
Eivissa–Portinatx road to
Santa Gertrudis continues
to Port de Sant Miquel

Cova de Ca'n Marça

Port de Sant Miquel, at the end of the road

33 47 76

Etr–Oct 10:30–7

The San Miguel (£) at Sant Miquel

None

Moderate

Above: *the beach at Portinatx, one of the busiest on Ibiza's northern coast*

PORT DE SANT MIQUEL ⭐

This deep-cut inlet of the northern coast is an excellent natural harbour and has a white sand beach. On the inlet's eastern side (right-hand as you look out to sea) there are several futuristic hotels – the Hotel Clubs Cartago, Galeon and San Miquel. Steps up to these offer excellent platforms for photographers wanting shots of the bay.

Close to Port de Sant Miquel is the Hacienda Na Xamena (➤ 101), the only hotel on the island with a five-star rating. It is also one of the most attractive, and has one of the island's best restaurants.

On the same side of the bay, beyond the hotels, are the Cova de Ca'n Marça, caves that were once used by smugglers as stores for contraband. Excavations have revealed animal bones, mostly of rodents, but no firm evidence for occupation by man.

Today the caves are open to the public, clever use of light adding considerably to the natural beauty of the stalagmites and stalactites.

> ### Did you know ?
>
> In 1929 King Alfonso XIII came ashore at Cala de Portinatx for a short break from the rigours of reviewing his navy. To celebrate, the town immediately changed its name to Portinatx del Rey (the King's Portinatx). Under Franco's regime the extra words were dropped from the name, but despite the restoration of the monarchy and an official visit to Ibiza by King Juan Carlos in 1994, the town's name has not yet returned to its royal form.

PORTINATX ✪

It could be strongly argued that the village (pronounced 'Port-e-natch') is the happy medium of tourism: enough development to support the local economy, but not so overpowering that the essential beauty of the place – which is, after all, one of the major reasons that tourists come – is destroyed. Though there are tourist hotels and apartments, there is still a fringe of pine and juniper to Portinatx's beautiful half-moon cove, famed for its shallow waters, where many ships were able to ride out a storm. In former times, the Barbary Corsairs and other pirates also knew of the benefits of the cove, as the watchtower on the headland named for it (Punta sa Torre, on the western side of the bay) indicates.

The tower is a good objective for a walk, as is the headland on the eastern side of the bay with a path hugging the cliff edge all the way to Punta Moscarter.

Those looking for equally fine views, but of, rather than from, the cliffs can hire boats at Portinatx. A boat trip westward, passing Cala Xarraca (► 49) to reach the very remote coast near Cap Blanc, is especially rewarding.

✚	29D5
⊠	Northern tip of Ibiza, at the end of the main C733 road from Eivissa
🍴	Lots of restaurants (£–£££)
🚌	Buses from Eivissa
♿	Reasonable

PUIG DE MISSA ✪✪✪

This curious little hill (► 24) stands on the western outskirts of Santa Eulària, the church at its top accessible by a corkscrew road. The hill itself is charming for its church and houses which top it, but is chiefly visited for the view it offers of the town and local coast. Try to visit during the evening when the softer, orange-tinged light creates a magical view of Santa Eulària and the hilltop buildings.

Close to the church is the **Barrau Museum**, which houses a collection of paintings of the Catalan artist Laureà Barrau, who died in 1957.

Below: *Puig de Missa, with its 16th-century church and cluster of houses*

✚	29D4
🚌	Eivissa–Santa Eulària; the bus does not go right to the top of the hill
🍴	La Posada, (££) signed from Avenida Padre Guasch

Barrau Museum

⊠	Puig de Missa
🕐	May–Sep Sun 10–noon
♿	None
💷	Cheap

PUNTA ARABÍ ✪

In the 1960s, with the rise of Flower Power and hippy culture, the youth of the western world sought their own Utopia. In the USA they found it on the west coast of California, but in Europe it was found in what seemed a most unlikely place – Ibiza. Franco's Spain was not the most liberal country in Europe, far from it in fact, but Ibiza was a backwater of Spain, an island a long way off. Franco's repressions caused major waves in Madrid, but by the time the waves had reached Ibiza they were minor ripples. There was another factor, too. The Ibizenco were a cosmopolitan folk, their history saw to that, and as a result they were philosophical about new settlers. If you could pay your way, you were OK.

The first hippies chanced upon Dalt Vila, relishing its ancient, unsophisticated feel. They smoked marijuana on the beach, listened to loud music and spoke endlessly of the new Utopia. Attracted by this European scene, the rich and famous followed. Then came those who saw in this gathering the possibility of making money. Discos and bars opened and Ibiza changed forever. The real hippies ignored the new commercialism, moving north towards San Carlos. They maintained their clothing and their ideals, funding their lifestyle by running the hippy market at Club Punta Arabí, a 'village' named after the sharp, eastern pointing headland near by. Now, every Wednesday, the market attracts coachloads. Go to savour the last embers of the '60s fire.

+ 29D4
✉ Sandwiched between Es Canar and S'Argamassa, near Santa Eulària
🍴 Lots of choice (£–£££)
🚌 Buses from Santa Eulària
♿ Reasonable, but crowded

The hippy market at Punta Arabí, more popular than ever

PUNTA GROSSA ✪✪

Viewpoints on the cliffs of Punta Grossa – particularly at the road end, but beware, the cliffs are sheer and unprotected – offer marvellous vistas to Cala de Sant Vicenç, to the south, and the curiously named Clot des Llamp to the north.

Cala de Sant Vicenç is one of Ibiza's more recently developed bays and the building has not always been as sympathetic as it might have been. That said, the bay is still beautiful when viewed from the headland, and the beach and facilities on offer are excellent. The nearby town of Sant Vicenç de sa Cala (San Vicente) is a straggle of whitewashed houses beside a fine church and is beautifully sited below pine-clad hills – reminders of the Greek name for Ibiza and Formentera – the Pine Islands.

Close to Clot des Llamp, and reached by a sometimes difficult trek, is a cave whose excavated interior revealed objects even older than Ibiza's Greek name. In Carthaginian times the Cova des Culleram was a shrine to Tanit, the Punic goddess of the underworld, who is usually portrayed as a lion. Hundreds of clay figures of Tanit have been found in the cave, together with other objects in gold, and heaps of ashes and charred bone. It is thought that funeral rites were carried out at the cave, the families of the dead making offerings to Tanit to ensure safe passage to the after-life for their loved ones. The best of the finds from the cave can be seen at the Archaeological Museum in Eivissa (➤ 36).

✚ 29E5
✉ Punta Grossa is the headland in the northeastern corner of Ibiza, reached by a winding road from Cala de Sant Vicenç
🍴 None
🚌 Not on a bus route
♿ Inaccessible

Above: *looking towards Punta Grossa from Sant Vicenç*

✚ 28B2

✉ The road from Eivissa to the island's airport reaches a turning to the right just before the main airport buildings. Turn right here, then left, at the unmarked village of Es Codolar, along a road signed for Cala Jondal

🍴 Limited choice (£–££)

🚌 Not on a bus route

♿ Few; access difficult, but not impossible

SA CALETA ✪

In the history of Ibiza, Sa Caleta is famous as one of the two original Phoenician sites on the island, the other being at Eivissa. Phoenician Sa Caleta, however, was inhabited for as little as 40 years or so, and seems never to have been much more than a settlement peopled by shipwrights and other workers. When it was abandoned, all Phoenician interest in Ibiza was concentrated at Eivissa.

Today Sa Caleta is a delightful cove, its picturesque qualities enhanced by the scattering of fishermen's huts, all that remain of a small, but once thriving, fishing port.

To the west is the curious headland of Punta Jondal, a skeletal finger of rock poking out into the Mediterranean. The rock of the headland and Fita des Jondal, the hillock which separates Sa Caleta from Cala Jondal, is a beautiful golden brown, a fine contrast with the green pines that top the cliffs and the clear blue waters. Cala Jondal itself is popular despite its apparent isolation. It has pebbles as well as sand, and a good restaurant set among cedars. From it Platja Virgen (the Virgin Beach) is signed. The beach is rather better known than the name would imply.

On the other side of Sa Caleta is Platja des Codolar, a rocky beach situated right at the end of the airport runway. Depending upon your point of view this is either entertaining or an ear-splitting nuisance. What is undeniable is that the beach offers excellent views towards Es Vedrá (➤ 55), to the west, and Cap des Falcó to the east.

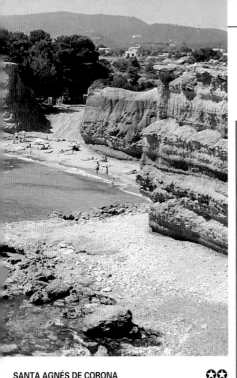

Sa Caleta: there is little to see today of the fishing port that once flourished here

SANTA AGNÉS DE CORONA ✪✪

Santa Agnés de Corona (Santa Inés) is one of the most remote villages on Ibiza. Set among the uplands known as Es Amunts and close to the most inhospitable part of the coast, the village has retained its Ibizan character despite its apparent closeness to the fleshpots of Sant Antoni.

The peak of Puig d'en Serra lies just to the south, while the even higher peak of Cova is a little way northeastwards; the village is approached between almond orchards, the trees growing in startling red-brown soil.

The church, built in the early years of the last century, stands in the main square. On the wall facing the village square is a statue of an Agnus Dei, or Lamb of God, perhaps a play on the village saint's name? Here you will find what few concessions there are to modern Ibiza – a good restaurant and a few local crafts for sale.

From close to the village dirt roads head for the coast and towards the hills. On the coast the rugged cliffs around Cap Negret offer spectacular views (especially to the islands of Ses Margalides) as you walk the coastal path, though care is needed as the path is very rocky and the cliffs here are among the highest on the island.

North of the village the coast towards Cap des Mossons is as remote as it is possible to be on the island. If you are tempted this way be sure to be equipped with good walking shoes or boots and, above all, a good supply of water.

✚ 28B4

✉ One of the most picturesque drives in Ibiza heads northwards from Sant Antoni along a road which runs parallel to the coast to reach Sant Miquel. The first village along this road – a short detour off the road is required – is Santa Agnés

🍽 One tiny bar/café (£)

🚌 Infrequent bus service

♿ Reasonable

✚ 28B3
✉ 16km from Eivissa, at the other end of the C731
🍴 Lots of choices (£–£££)
🚌 Regular bus service

Aquarium Cap Blanc
✉ Cova de ses Llegostes, Cala Grassió
🕐 Apr–Sep daily 10–6
🍴 Novedad (££), Cala Grassió
🚌 Not on a bus route
♿ Few
👜 Moderate

A modern sculpture at the southern end of Sant Antoni

SANT ANTONI DE PORTMANY   ✪✪

Sant Antoni de Portmany (San Antonio), Ibiza's second largest town, could hardly be more different from Eivissa. Yet for all its brash modernity, it is an historically interesting town, one whose development mirrors the development of the island as a whole.

To the north of the town, beyond Cala Salada, is the Cova des Vi (Cave of Des Vi) where dynamic cave paintings were discovered in 1917. Doubts still remain about the exact age of the paintings, some experts maintaining that they are Bronze Age in origin and therefore dating from about 2,000 BC. Others believe that they were the work of Carthaginian soldiers manning a look-out and therefore no older than 600 BC. If they are indeed Bronze Age, the caves are one of the earliest signs of human habitation on the island. The cave is not open to the public, but as it is closed only by an iron grill the paintings are quite visible.

When the army of King Jaime took Ibiza, wresting the island from its Moorish settlers, Christianity was established as the major faith. Near the road to Cala Salada, closer to Sant Antoni than the Des Vi cave, the Capilla de Santa Agnés, an underground chapel discovered in 1917, dates from this early Christian period. The chapel was restored in the early 1980s and can be visited.

Perhaps because of the existence of this early chapel, in 1305 the Bishop of Tarragon gave permission for a church and consecrated cemetery of Sant Antoni. That church, dedicated to St Anthony and so giving the town its name, is one of the oldest in Ibiza. It was built on the site of a Moorish mosque and incorporates some architectural details it presumably borrowed from its predecessor, as well as the more typical fortress-like looks of its day.

For many years Sant Antoni was a fishing port, and one link with those days can be found at Cala Grassió a little way to the north. There the Cova de ses Llegostes, a natural fish pool, was used by the local fishermen to keep excess fish fresh while they waited for market. Today the cave has been turned into a natural **aquarium** which can be visited.

Sant Antoni had developed into a small town when the 1960s and 1970s

ushered in the era of mass tourism. Virtually overnight – and it is easy to underestimate just how fast the growth of Sant Antoni was: it was phenomenal – the town was transformed into the island's major package-holiday centre, exemplifying all that was both good and bad in tourism. While the development of hotels, bars, discos, souvenir shops and the like brought enormous economic benefits to some of the townsfolk, it was at the expense of a landscape that had once been among the finest on the island.

Aquarium Cap Blanc, near Sant Antoni

A Walk Around the Punta de Ses Portes

Distance
8km

Time
3 hours

Start/end point
The car park at Es Cavallet beach (Platja des Cavallet)
➕ 28C2

Lunch
La Escollera (£)
✉ Es Cavallet beach

This walk begins on Ibiza's official nudist beach, so be prepared for strange looks as you pass by, particularly if you are carrying a camera with a long lens!

From the car park walk down to the beach and turn right, heading for the watchtower at the far end.

Walking on the beach is difficult, but the going can be made a little easier by keeping to the firmer sand which is near the water's edge. Alternatively, you could cross the sand dunes at the back of the beach to reach an easier track.

Whichever route you choose to follow, you will eventually reach the watchtower on Punta de ses Portes.

The first tower was built in the late 16th or early 17th century to protect the rich fishing off the headland, but was abandoned when the trade became uneconomic. Rebuilt in the mid-18th century as one of the string of coastal towers, the watchtower was finally abandoned in the 19th century.

The name of the headland means the 'Cape of the Gates', the three offshore islets creating passages or 'gates' between Ibiza and Formentera.

A view of Es Cavallet, near the starting point of the walk

Now follow the easier path behind the beach of Platja de Migjorn and continue to the road at the far end. Turn right and follow the broad track beside the road to reach a roundabout. Continue straight on, walking parallel with the road.

On both sides now are the salt pans of Ibiza's salt industry (➤ 54).

Follow the road across a narrow causeway and soon afterwards turn right to follow the rough track that leads back to the car park at Es Cavallet.

SANT CARLES DE PERALTA ✪✪✪

This quiet, largely unspoilt village (▶ 25, Top Ten) is a tiny place – it takes less than five minutes to walk from one side to the other – but has some truly delightful corners. Look for the house (near the T-junction of roads to Cala Mastella and Cala de Sant Vicenç) that is blue rather than white, and for the new pedestrian, tiled walkway with its array of small shops selling books and locally made crafts.

Just outside the village, the **Museo es Trui de Ca'n Andreu** is a 17th-century house restored to its original state and decorated in period style.

SANTA EULÀRIA ✪✪✪

The modern seafront and harbour area of Santa Eulària (▶ 26) show it to be a prosperous town, yet, while embracing tourism, the town has not forgotten its past.

The old bridge – below Puig de Missa (▶ 24) – sits beside the modern crossing that takes the main road for Eivissa over the river. Though there is some dispute over its true origins, most experts agree that the bridge was built by the Romans. One local legend maintains that it was built by the Devil and that his efforts took only a single night. So strong was this belief that it is said that many locals declined to cross the bridge after nightfall. With its elegant arches, warm stone and the mass of reeds and oleander close by, it is certainly very picturesque. Near by a walkway has been built, complete with lights and welcome shady trees.

➕ 29D4

Museo es Trui de Ca'n Andreu

✉ A few metres off the road to Cala Mastella

🕐 Apr–Sep daily 10–1 & 3–6

🍴 The Plaza del Sol (££), in the Plaça del Sol close to the Baluarte des Portal Nou

🚌 Close to Sant Carles which is on the Santa Eulària–Es Figueral bus route

♿ None. The entrance to the museum from the car park is not negotiable by wheelchairs. However, further up the road, past the museum, there is a second entrance which is negotiable. The house itself can be negotiated on the ground floor

💶 Moderate

Santa Eulària

➕ 29D3

✉ On Ibiza's eastern coast a few kilometres north of Eivissa

🍴 Pizzeria Magu, towards the harbour end of the seafront

🚌 Santa Eulària is served by buses from all parts of the island

♿ Few

💶 Free

Santa Eulària's ancient bridge, built by the Romans – or by the Devil

SANTA GERTRUDIS ⭐
DE FRUITERA

Santa Gertrudis de Fruitera (its name derives from the local area's history of fruit growing) has a strong claim to lying at the centre of Ibiza, the point furthest from the sea. That fact has not stopped some recent development, however, though the old village remains a very pleasant place, retaining the peace and slow tempo of life of the surrounding countryside.

In the airy Plaça de la Iglesia stands the church, a square-cut, somewhat severe, 18th-century building with a distinctive yellow bell-gable. Santa Gertrudis' position has made it popular with artists and ex-patriates who favour living in rural Ibiza . As a result, the village shops and bars are well worth visiting. The Bar Costa is one of the most delightful of all Ibizan bars, with hams hanging from the ceiling. It claims to hold the record for sales of *bocadillos* (the typical Spanish sandwich) at over 500 in a day and is also an art gallery in its own right, the owner having, in time-honoured tradition, accepted paintings for drinks from penniless artists over the years.

There are several craft and antique shops ideal for browsing in the church square, while just outside the village – on the road to Sant Mateu – is Libro Azul, a bookshop and picture gallery.

➕ 28C4
✉ Take the C733 from Eivissa towards Portinatx then, after about 6km, turn left along the road to Sant Miquel
🍴 Lots of choice (£–£££)
♿ Reasonable

Above: *the bell-turret on the church at Santa Gertrudis*

Did you know ?

The typical Ibizan house (casament) is a thick-walled cube with small windows set so as to maximise light and ventilation, but to minimise the sun's penetration of the interior. A porch (porxet) offers a sheltered place to sit and to store fruit and vegetables. The flat roof is supported by pine logs and coated with clay and dried seaweed as a waterproofer. If more rooms are required, more cubes can easily be added.

A Ferry Trip Along the Northern Coast

Ibiza's northern coast is the island's most inaccessible. Drivable roads and tracks are few, most of the coastline being visited only by determined walkers.

A fine alternative to walking is to take a boat trip along the coast. There are several possibilities. Perhaps the best is to form a small group and rent a boat (there always seems to be a willing crowd at the harbour in Sant Antoni), the advantages of being your own master having to be set against the increased cost of such a trip. Alternatively, in summer there are regular ferry services from Sant Antoni to Portinatx. Some of these services are *ad hoc*, but one company (Cruceros Portmany ☎ 34 34 71) has started to run a regular scheduled service.

Leaving Sant Antoni, the first landmark is Cala Grassió, an overflow bay for the 'Sant Ant' crowds. Heading northwards, the boat rounds Cap Negret to reach Cala Salada. North again is Cap Nunó. Close to here is the painted Cova Des Vi (► 66). Beyond the headland is one of the wildest stretches of coast: look out for the huge cliffs of Joan Andreu which, at 365m, are the highest on the island. Beyond Cap Rubió are the cliffs of Es Portitxol, one of the loveliest places on the northern coast. Here you can also catch a glimpse of Hacienda Na Xamena, Ibiza's most luxurious hotel (► 101).

Beyond Punta de Sa Creu is Port de Sant Miquel and the busy beach of Benirrás, before passing a final wild section of the coast, including Cala Xarraca (► 49). Portinatx is now just ahead.

Distance
50km

Time
5 hours

Start point
Sant Antoni
✚ 28B3

End point
Portinatx
✚ 29D5

Lunch
Cas Mallorqui (£)
✉ Portinatx

Sunset at Cala Grassió, a short hop from the sprawl of Sant Antoni

✚ 28B3

✉ The main C731 road
takes visitors quickly
between Sant Antoni and
Eivissa. To the south of
that road is the highest
land on Ibiza. On the
southern flank of this
upland a fine road – start
by following the road to
the airport – offers a
slow, but more scenic,
route between the two
main towns. Sant Josep
is the largest village on
this road

🍴 Good range (£–££)

🚌 Regular bus service

♿ Reasonable

*Sant Josep, largely
untouched by the hustle
and bustle of tourism*

SANT JOSEP DE SA TALAIA ✪

The addition to the name of Sant Josep (San José)
indicates its position, close to the northern flank of Sa
Talaia, Ibiza's highest peak.

The village, set on a hillside above a fertile plain, the
surrounding hills covered in pines, is an idyllic place. It has
also escaped major development, though there are signif-
icant numbers of visitors, drawn by the craft shops and art
galleries as Sant Josep is a major centre for island-based
artists. El Palio and Siena at Esconellas 34 are the most
important galleries. Look, too, for shops selling
embroidery, most of it made by the local womenfolk.

Also worth looking out for is the village church, a
typically fortress-like building with an elegant arcaded
entrance. The church was started in the 15th century, but
not finally completed until 300 years later. Inside there is a
huge baroque altar complete with statues in niches. The
walls are beautifully half-tiled, the lavish ceiling bosses
equally good. Look, too, for the realistic, but gruesome,
painting of Christ after his scourging.

Sant Josep is the starting point for the walk (➤ 53) to
Ibiza's highest point and has several excellent refreshment
stops for weary walkers. There is also a quiet park,
opposite the church, for resting after your exertions.

SANT JOAN DE LABRITJA ⭐

Sant Joan de Labritja (San Juan Bautista or St John the Baptist in English) lies in one of Ibiza's most beautiful valleys, formed between the high peaks of the Serra de la Mala Costa, to the south, and, to the north, hills which slope down to cliffs above remote bays such as Cala de Serra and Port de Ses Caletes. The high point of the southern hills, Es Fornàs, is, at 410m, the third highest Ibizan peak. A dirt track leads up to the peak from the road that links Sant Joan to Sant Vicenç. It is a difficult drive and caution is needed, but the reward is a magnificent view over Ibiza's wild northeastern corner, and southwards across the island towards Eivissa.

For such a small town – little more than a village – Sant Joan has a surprising number of banks, perhaps reflecting its position as the chief town of one of Ibiza's administrative districts. The regional headquarters – the Ajuntament – is a lovely building. Opposite there is a quaint, and very unusual, terrace of balconied houses. The village highlight is the colonnaded 18th-century church with its distinctive bell-tower and tiled cupola. The church courtyard has been extended to include a raised square reached by steps.

 29D5

✉ 24km north of Eivissa, just off the C733 road to Portinatx

🍴 Limited choice (£–££)

🚌 The Portinatx buses stop in the village

♿ Reasonable, but steps up to church

Above: *the handsome church at Sant Joan, focal point of the village*

SANT MATEU D'AUBARCA ⭐

As with the nearby village of Santa Agnés (► 65), Sant Mateu d'Aubarca (San Mateo) lies in the upland region of Es Amunts and is similarly sandwiched between high peaks. The village consists of little more than a church and its square set on a hilltop, but it is wonderfully picturesque. The surrounding hills are clothed in pines, though close to the village there is fertile farmland where sheep and goats graze.

The church was built in the 18th century and has a fine gallery. Two homely touches are the local children's model of the village and the birds nesting in the roof of the entrance porch.

From the village, close to the church, a forest track heads north towards the sea, deteriorating as it nears Cap des Mossons and the magnificent Cala d'Aubarca some 4km (2 miles) away.

Cala d'Aubarca is regarded by many as the most beautiful spot on the northern coast and is certainly one of the quietest and most spectacular. If you are visiting by car, leave your vehicle well short of the cliff edge, which is unstable. Be prepared for a steep scramble down to the beach.

✚ 28C4
✉ The road from Sant Antoni along the coast passes Santa Agnés, then continues to Sant Mateu. An alternative approach to the village is from the south: take the C733 towards Portinatx, then bear left on the road to Sant Miquel. At Santa Gertrudis turn left and follow the road through to Sant Mateu
🍴 One bar
🚌 The village is not on a bus route
♿ Reasonable

Above: *Sant Mateu's church*
Opposite: *restoration work in the church at Sant Miquel (top) which lies inland from Port de Sant Miquel (below)*

Did you know ?

Although there are few wild animals on Ibiza there is one unique domesticated one – Ca Eivissenc, the Ibizan dog – and the country area around San Mateo is where you are likely to see one. The dog looks a bit like a stubby greyhound, but with its big ears and long snout it is also very similar to the sacred dogs of ancient Egypt.

It is believed that the dogs were brought to the island by either the Carthaginians or the Phoenicians, who used them as hunting dogs. Years of inbreeding means that though they are good-looking, amiable animals, they are notoriously stupid.

SANT MIQUEL DE BALANSAT ✪✪

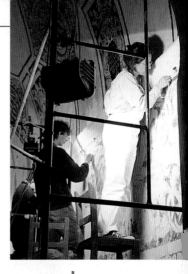

Try to visit Sant Miquel de Balansat (San Miguel) on a late Thursday afternoon when the square in front of the church fills with local people who perform Ibizan folk dances to the music of an authentic folk band. The meaning of most of the dances are lost in time, but many seem to relate to courtship. Some of the performers wear traditional costume, the men clothed in red hats, bandannas and cummerbunds, black jackets and baggy white trousers, the women in long, black or white pleated skirts with aprons, long shawls and mantillas. The women also braid their hair and wear ornate necklaces showing a distinct Moorish influence. Although basically similar, the costumes are very individual and if visitors inquire, the reasons for the subtle differences will be explained, usually in terms of family history. This colourful display ends with the passing of a *porrón* (► 99) and, of course, the handing round of a hat.

The church is a fine 14th-century building, one of the oldest on the island, though the porch and patio are later. Inside, the 17th-century wall paintings in the Chapel Benirràs are undergoing a careful programme of restoration. They are one of the few examples of their type on the island.

✚ 28C4

✉ About 4km from Eivissa a road branches left from the C733 (the road to Portinatx) passing through Santa Gertrudis to reach Sant Miquel and, beyond, the port of the same name

🍽 Lots of choices (£–££)

🚌 There are regular buses from Eivissa

♿ Reasonable, but church is at top of long steep hill

A quiet corner of Sant Rafel, a village astride the busy Eivissa to Sant Antoni road

SANT RAFEL DE FORCO ✪

The drive to Sant Rafel (San Rafael) from Eivissa passes through beautiful country, with orange groves on both sides of the road. Unfortunately the sheer volume of traffic and the somewhat eccentric (not to say dangerous) driving of too many travellers mean that the scenery is missed by most drivers.

The village church of Sant Rafel, a graceful building, its lines reminiscent of mainland churches, dates from the 19th century. From it there is a marvellous view of Dalt Vila.

Sant Rafel appeals to all Ibiza's visitors, but the attractions are quite diverse. Some come because the village is the island's major production centre for ceramics. Much of the output from the ceramic factories can be seen in any of Ibiza's many souvenir shops, but there are also craft potters in the village, their work standing comparison with that of any of the island's artists.

Long after the potteries have closed (indeed, not many hours before they open) the other major Sant Rafel tourist attraction opens its doors. This is Privilege, Ibiza's most famous disco. Privilege gained status as Ku, the change of name having made no difference to either its position in the disco hierarchy or its shows. With its internationally famous DJs, its swimming pool, fountain and amazing light show – not to mention the more usual disco delights

+ 28B3

Did you know?

The world population of Eleonora's falcon is estimated at no more than 5,500 pairs, perhaps as few as 4,000. The birds nest on the rocky islands and cliffs of the Mediterranean, with as many as 80 pairs breeding on Ibiza. Visitors are most likely to see them on the island's southern uplands and cliffs, though they have also been seen in the north of the island and in the uplands around Sant Mateo. The falcons, a little smaller than peregrine falcons, hunt birds and insects and are a magnificent sight.

SERRA GROSSA ●●

Technically, Serra Grossa refers to the island's largest area of unspoilt upland, which lies between the C731, the main road linking Eivissa and Sant Antoni, and the road from Eivissa to Sant Josep. However, the following information applies equally well to the uplands south of Sant Joan and those near Sant Mateu.

The typical cover of Ibiza's upland areas is a forest of Aleppo pine, though the pine stands are sometimes interspersed with escaped cultivated trees – almond, fig, carob and olive. Aleppo pine has a very thin needle, the easier to survive summer's hot sun, and so casts little shadow. Beneath it, therefore, numerous flowers and shrubs thrive, the most obvious being Mediterranean heath (*Erica multiflora*). However, in places where natural or man-made fires have destroyed the forest and overgrazing has impoverished the soil, there are areas of 'degraded' forest where lavender, southern grape hyacinth and various other colourful plants bloom. Lower down the hillsides where ancient cultivated terraces have been allowed to return to the wild, gladioli, chrysanthemums, grape hyacinths and poppies thrive.

The beautiful country of the Serra Grossa, typical of Ibiza's upland landscape

Formentera

Swing a map of Formentera about half a turn and squint your eyes, and you can convince yourself that the blueprint for the island was a seahorse. From the straight spine followed by the Via Major, the seahorse's rolled tail follows the eastern coastline from Punta Roja past La Mola to Punta Palmera, while the head points towards Cap de Barbaría.

The usual explanation of Formentera's name is that it derives from 'wheat', the island having been one of Rome's granaries. Yet that seems so unlikely on this arid outcrop that many experts believe the name must derive from an ancient word for a headland, the two headlands of Barbaría and La Mola (the head and tail of the seahorse) being such prominent features of an otherwise flat island.

Formentera is a quiet, peaceful place, the ideal antidote to the hectic activity of tourist Ibiza. Come here to relax if you have been burning the candle at both ends on the larger island.

'Te molt poca cosa
que veure.'

(There is very little to see)

Saying popular with Formentera's locals; said, presumably, to keep visitors away as it is entirely false.

Getting to Formentera

Flebasa/Trasmapi Ferries

✉ Estación Maritima,
Eivissa, Ibiza

☎ 31 40 05/31 20 71

✉ Estación Maritima, La
Savina, Formentera

☎ 32 29 30

Umafisa Lines

✉ 17 Avenida Santa Eulària,
Eivissa, Ibiza

☎ 31 45 13/31 44 86

✉ Estación Maritima, La
Savina, Formentera

☎ 32 30 07

Only 4km separate Punta de ses Portes, the most southerly point on Ibiza, from the northern tip of S'Espalmador, the island off Formentera's northern shore. Since the sea between S'Espalmador and Trucadors, Formentera's northern tip, can be waded on calm days, it might seem a simple thing to cross between Ibiza and the smaller island. Yet Es Freus, the passage between the islands, with its numerous islands, sand banks and strong currents, has always been a difficult passage for ships.

Today's traveller has no such problems: numerous boats leave Eivissa's harbour for Formentera every day during the summer months. Of these boats the most reliable are the scheduled services of Flebasa/Trasmapi, which include both passenger and car ferries, and the Umafisa car ferry. The Flebasa/Trasmapi passenger services are by fast catamarans which cut the journey time of the slow ferries (about one hour) in half. Tickets can be bought at the Estación Maritima on Eivissa's harbour (on the side nearest the new town, not at the large building beside the monument to the Corsairs), at the harbourside Estación Maritima at La Savina on Formentera, or on the boat itself. Check the return times of boats and remember to arrive early if you are planning to catch the last boat as it might be full. Those taking a day trip to Formentera from Ibiza at the height of summer would be advised to catch an earlier boat back, just to be sure.

Leaving from Eivissa, the boat offers a wonderful view of Dalt Vila and Ibiza's southeastern coast and soon passes the lighthouse on the islets of Penjats and Porcs to reach the long, flat S'Espalmador (▶ 84), its watchtower prominently visible. If you are travelling on the deck of the catamaran rather than in the comfortable seats inside, look out for seabirds: Cory's shearwater and the Balearic subspecies of the Manx shearwater are often seen on the journey.

On the catamaran across to Formentera, a trip of about half an hour

The Beaches of Formentera

Formentera is a quieter, more peaceful island than Ibiza, better for visitors looking for relaxing days on the beach, a good meal and an evening stroll rather than a hectic nightlife. It is therefore popular with families and has beaches to meet all expectations. Except at the cliff-bordered ends of the islands, it is possible to swim almost anywhere, but the major beaches are listed below.

Llevant ✚ 29E2
On the eastern side of the Trucadors peninsula. More weatherswept than the western side, so occasionally has real breakers. Popular with nudists. Swimming is good on calmer days. Facilities are reasonable, but decreasing as you move towards S'Espalmador.

Ses Illetes, one of the typically flat, sandy beaches of Formentera

Ses Illetes ✚ 29E2
On the western, more sheltered, side of Trucadors. Formentera's official nudist beach. Good facilities.

Es Pujols ✚ 29E2
Excellent beach close to one of the island's major tourist areas. Excellent facilities. See also ➤ 85.

Cala Savina ✚ 29D2
Close to La Savina. Too close for some as it is the easiest for day-trippers to reach, though the facilities are good.

Cala Saona ✚ 29D1
A small beach in a beautiful cove. Excellent facilities. See also ➤ 83.

Platja de Tramuntana ✚ 29E1
On the northern edge of the thin piece of land linking La Mola and the rest of the island. Long enough to offer privacy, but can be weatherswept. Reasonable facilities.

Platja de Migjorn ✚ 29E1
A huge and very beautiful beach, with clean white sand and equally clean blue water. Understandably popular, but big enough to absorb vast crowds. Excellent facilities.

29D1

Cap de Barbaría lies at the end of the road which heads south from Sant Françesc

None

In summer there are regular buses

None

What to See in Formentera

CAP DE BARBARÍA

The road from Sant Françesc to Cap de Barbaría, the southern tip of Formentera, is a good introduction to the landscapes of the island. After leaving the modern buildings of the town behind there are just a few scattered farms – some sheep and goats and the odd cultivated field – but the country soon becomes more arid, burnt out by the sun and wind.

Close to Cap de Barbaría, just off the road, are three prehistoric sites, all dating from about 2000 BC. Closest to the headland is a stone circle, though the few remaining stones are not easily distinguished from the natural rocks. Next are the remains of several dwellings, the ground plan much more obvious than the stone circle, and finally the remains of another settlement. The sites are protected by fencing, but can easily be seen through the grills.

The empty lighthouse marks the journey's end. Here, as at La Mola (➤ 22), the cliff edge is abrupt and unforgiving: please take care, especially if you have children with you.

If you stand at the tip of the headland and gaze southwards, the next land, about 220km away, is Africa's northern coast. Head along the eastern edge of the cape to reach Torre des Garroveret, a well-preserved watchtower dating from the mid-18th century. The area around the tower – and on the walk from the lighthouse – is the preserve of goats and the famous green lizards of Formentera (➤ 13).

Feral goats graze by the old watchtower at Cap de Barbaría

CALA SAONA ✪✪

Just a couple of kilometres to the west of Sant Françesc, Cala Saona is the most commercial of Formentera's bays. It is also one of the loveliest, its turquoise waters and beach framed by red cliffs and backed by pine trees, the tourist sites neatly positioned. It is an excellent place to swim and a good starting point for walks to quieter parts of the coast.

Head north for a quiet cliff-top walk, perhaps going as far as Punta se Sa Gavina and another well-preserved watchtower. Torre se Sa Gavina, built in the late 18th century is, unusually for the Pine Islands, open. Alternatively, head west to Punta Rasa and on to Costa des Bou where solitude is almost assured.

✚ 29D1
🍴 Various choices (£–£££)
♿ Reasonable

Above: Ca-na Costa, an important indication of Bronze Age settlement on the islands

CA-NA COSTA ✪

In the late 1970s an amateur archaeologist exploring the eastern edge of Estany Pudent (➤ 23), the larger of the two salty lakes to the north of Sant Françesc, discovered the megalithic remains of Ca-na Costa. The site is being carefully excavated, but can be visited. So far, finds have included human remains, pottery and jewellery, together with axes that date the site to the Bronze Age to about 4,000 years ago.

Ca-na Costa is an unusually complex site for its period, and is now recognised as one of the most important sites on the Balearic Islands. It seems likely that Bronze Age man found a forested island but that their slash and burn agriculture destroyed the forests, allowing the fertile top soil to be sun-baked and blown away. By the time the Greeks and Romans came it was a strategic outpost rather than the welcoming, fertile paradise the builders of Ca-na Costa had known.

✚ 29E2
🕐 Open access at all times
🍴 None
♿ Few

29E2
None
Possible
Ferries leave La Savina
several times daily

S'ESPALMADOR

From Punta de ses Portes, the southern tip of Ibiza, a chain of islets and rocks points the way to Trucadors, the northernmost tip of Formentera. Only one of these islets is big enough to be habitable, or even worth visiting – S'Espalmador, the islet closest to Formentera.

Trucadors is a curious finger of land, little more than sand dunes dotted with patches of grass and spiky shrubs, and narrowing beaches. It is an excellent place for sunbathing and swimming and, if the sea is calm and can be guaranteed to remain so, for visiting S'Espalmador. The island lies just 200m or so from Trucadors' sandy end and the sea can be waded. Most visitors, however, choose the less precarious option of a boat ride.

The privately owned island, which is uninhabited, has some excellent beaches. The bay of Port de S'Espalmador, on the southwestern coast, is a particular favourite with the Spanish royal family. From it, a track leads to the northern tip for a view of the nearby islet of Porcs', passing the recently restored watchtower known as Sa Guardiola – the money box. Strong swimmers might be tempted to believe that on a good day they could cross the straits ahead to the mainland. However, they should recall the name of this stretch of water – Es Freus, the difficult passage.

Sun, sea and sand in plenty at S'Espalmador – but little else

ES PUJOLS ✪

Es Pujols and Cala Saona are the major tourist developments on Formentera. Within easy reach of the village are fine beaches: Platja des Pujols close to the village, where fishing boats are still pulled on to the sand, and those on the low headland of Trucadors. The latter include Ses Illetes, Formentera's only official nude beach, though there are as many unofficial nude beaches as there are nudists in search of a quiet stretch of sand. The facilities on Es Pujols' beaches are simpler than on Ibiza, but that is in keeping with the slower pace of life on the smaller island.

To the east of the village is the promontory of Punta Prima. Here, as on many of Formentera's headlands, there is an 18th-century watchtower, though this one is being gradually overshadowed by tourist hotels. This is sad, as it is arguably the only place on the island where the modern development has been less than sympathetic. But that is a minor criticism: with its old fishermen's huts and a view across Estany Pudent to Ibiza's southern coast, with Es Vedrá prominent, Es Pujols is still an excellent place.

> ### Did you know ?
>
> *After the hippy invasion of Ibiza in the 1960s the Spanish police, the Guardia Civil, began to raid places where they suspected marijuana was being smoked. Some of the hippies retreated to Formentera, taking up residence at San Fernando. At the time Formentera's police only had bicycles at their disposal and the village was far enough away from Sant Françesc for the hippies to make an orderly retreat if needs be. It is said that in an attempt to overcome the time delay, the police made drugs raids in the island's taxis.*

✚ 29E2
✉ Lies on the other side of the Estany Pudent lagoon from La Savina, where most visitors to Formentera arrive. Roads circle the lagoon so the village can be reached either directly from La Savina, or from Sant Françesc by way of Sant Ferran
🍴 Various choices
♿ Reasonable

Above: *one of Formentera's two main tourist beaches, Platja des Pujols*

A Walk on Formentera's Wild Shore

Distance
7km

Time
3 hours

Start point
Cami de Sa Cala, El Pilar
✚ 29F1

End point
El Pilar Church
✚ 29F1

Lunch
El Mirador (£)
✉ On the main road (Via Major) between Sant Françesc & El Pilar, towards the top of the long hill
☎ 32 70 37

Though this fine walk can be a little difficult to follow on occasions, there is ample reward for perseverance.

At the western (Sant Françesc) end of the village, near the end of the 50kph limit and village signs, Cami de Sa Cala, signed as a footpath, heads northwards.

Follow this rough track to a fork. Branch left and continue to a sharp left bend. Turn right here, going through a makeshift gate and continue alongside a ruined wall. When the wall ends the path soon reaches another wall, low but complete. The cliff-top route lies on the other side of this: cross carefully and head across the scrub to reach a vague path occasionally marked with small cairns. Turn right.

At the cliff edge to the left lies Cova des Fum, the cave of smoke. Legend has it that here pirates gathered the local Moors and then killed them by lighting fires that filled the caves with smoke.

The vague path returns to the wall you climbed earlier and which separates a pleasant wood from the cliff. Continue to reach a crossing wall with steps. Head eastwards into woodland then bear left along a path towards the sea. Go over a wall at a wall junction, head eastwards again and climb a final wall. Continue ahead to reach the cliff edge close to Racó de sa Creu. Now follow a rough path which follows the shallow valley of the Torrent de sa Fontanella, soon reaching a wider track waymarked with red arrows. Pass houses, then follow a more obvious track to reach the road at El Pilar. Turn right to pass the church and follow the main road back to the start point.

The green lizards on Formentera are larger than those seen on Ibiza and can often be spotted on coastal rocks

LA MOLA ✪✪✪

The lighthouse at the headland (► 22) is La Mola's most prominent feature, but many visitors will be surprised to learn that it has another claim to fame: there is also a memorial to Jules Verne here. The great science-fiction writer had a habit of setting his stories against a background of actual geographical features, and La Mola features in *Hector Servadac or the Journey Around the Solar System*.

The road to the headland passes through the scattered village of El Pilar, from where a short rough track heads south to La Moli Vell de la Molathe, the Mola windmill. This fine old corn mill was built in 1778 and is still in regular use, making it the oldest functioning windmill on the Pine Islands. Close to the windmill is the church of El Pilar, a fine late-18th century building.

Finally, at the bottom of the steep hill that rises to the La Mola plateau, Es Caló, on the northern shore, is worth visiting. This tiny fishing village shelters beneath a huge, imposing crag and from it an old Roman road – the Camino Romano, which is signposted and can be followed – runs parallel to the shore.

LAS SALINAS ✪✪✪

Formentera's saltwater lagoons (► 23) are one of the most important wildlife habitats in the Balearics. Currently they are the centre of a controversy as to whether they should be developed to enhance the island's tourist industry, or whether a national park should be set up to preserve their unique environment for the future.

➕ 29F1
✉ The extreme eastern end of Formentera
🍴 Es Puig (£), at the end of the road, near the lighthouse
🚌 Sant Ferran–La Mola
♿ None
🎫 Free

Below: *restoration work being undertaken on the La Mola windmill*

➕ 29E2
✉ Estany des Peix and Estany Pudent lie each side of the La Savina–Sant Françesc road
🍴 None close to the lagoons, but many in the nearby towns of Es Pujols, Sant Françesc de Formentera and La Savina, for example the Casa Rafael (££), ✉ 14 Carrer d'Isidor Macabich, Sant Françesc
🚌 Es Pujols–Sant Françesc–La Savina
♿ None
🎫 Free

The beach at La Savina – as near as you can get to the island's arrival point

✚ 29D2
✉ Northern coast of the island
🍴 Various choices (£–£££)
♿ Reasonable

LA SAVINA ⭐

The ferry boats from Ibiza to Formentera have their terminus at La Savina (La Sabina), Formentera's only harbour. It takes its name from the Phoenician word for the juniper which still grows throughout the island. Formentera has no airport, so most visitors' first view of the island is of La Savina, its architecture making it seem more of a North African port than a European one.

Despite its exotic appearance, La Savina is a functioning harbour, many of its buildings catering solely for the passengers and freight arriving from Ibiza and mainland ports. It is, though, the site of one of Formentera's most delightful festivals, that of Our Lady of the Sea, held annually in July. Then the island's fishing boats gather here before sailing out to be blessed.

It is at La Savina that visitors can hire bicycles, scooters and even cars to explore the island. From the harbour, Via Major leads inland between the two salty lagoons that are such a notable feature of Formentera. Soon a road leads off left, taking the northern shore of Estany Pudent to reach Es Pujols (► 85). Soon after a right turn leads to Cala Saona (► 83). Turn right again off this road towards Punta de Sa Pedrera. The headland itself (Formentera at its wildest) can only be reached by a short walk. The area was quarried by the Moors, but a recent attempt to develop it was defeated by local opposition: there may only be rocks and a clear blue sea, but the islanders like it that way.

Opposite: *the centre of Sant Françesc, Formentera's unspoilt capital*

SANT FRANÇESC DE FORMENTERA ✪

Sant Françesc de Formentera (San Francisco Javier) is a complete contrast to Ibiza's capital of Eivissa. It is smaller, with only around 1,000 inhabitants, quieter and seems almost to be blinking at the strange sights tourism has brought it. Little seems to have changed here for centuries and it is to be hoped that the inevitable future tourist development will not change the town's lovely character.

In Carrer d'Eivissa the old church – known as Sa Tanca Vella – dates back to the 14th century, though it was carefully restored in the mid-1980s after the farmhouse into which it had been incorporated was demolished. The church in the town's main square is an extraordinary building. Erected in the 1780s, it was fortified, as on Ibiza, as a retreat in the event of a pirate attack. But whereas on Ibiza the fortification is rarely at the expense of graceful lines, here it created a bunker seemingly more suited to a nuclear than a cutlass attack. Close by is the privately owned **Museo Etnològic** (Ethnological Museum) with a collection of traditional island crafts and tools.

An excursion from the village is to the **Cuevas de Xeroni** – the Xeroni Caves – close to Sant Ferran. The caves were discovered in 1975 when a well was being dug. The approach to the caves and the entrance itself are hardly enough to make the pulse race with anticipation, but the caves do have good stalagmites and stalactites.

➕ 29D1
✉ Sant Françesc is Formentera's main town and administrative centre

Museo Etnològic
✉ Carrer de Santa Maria, Sant Françesc
🕐 May–Sep. Check at the Tourist Office as times are subject to variations
🍴 Casa Rafael (£), Carrer d'Isidor Macabich, Sant Françesc
🚍 La Savina–San Françesc
♿ None 💲 Cheap

Cuevas de Xeroni
✉ Beside Via Major, near Sant Ferran
🕐 May–Sep. Check at the Tourist Office as times are subject to variation
🍴 Casa Rafael, Carrer d'Isidor Macabich, Sant Françesc (£)
🚍 La Savina–Sant Françesc
♿ None 💲 Cheap

A Cycle Ride Across Formentera

Distance
38km return

Time
6 hours

Start/end point
La Savina
✚ 29D2

Lunch
El Mirador (£)
✉ On the climb up to
La Mola, 13.5km from
La Savina (5.5km from
La Mola)
☎ 32 70 37

The island is small enough to be crossed by bicycle in one day, and it is also the cheapest way to travel about. Cycles can be hired in La Savina. The section of the ride uphill to the La Mola plateau (➤ 22) is steep and unforgiving.

From La Savina take Via Major, the main island road, towards Sant Françesc (➤ 89) and continue straight ahead towards Sant Ferran (San Fernando) and Es Pujols (➤ 85).

Go through the outskirts of Sant Ferran (the main village lies just off the main road), ignoring the turns to the left (to Es Pujols) as you continue along Via Major. Ahead now the road is straight, but undulating, with a cycle track on each side.

At the 10km post a sign points to the Castellum Roma de Cans Pins, the excavated remains of a Roman defensive tower.

The hard work starts soon after the turn to Es Caló is reached, at 12km. Now the road ascends some 160m, initially a series of alpine-like windings.

Taking a breather in the main square of Sant Françesc

Eventually the gradient slackens, though it does not cease until 15km have been covered. Continue through pretty woodland to reach El Pilar where refreshment is available at the Bar Cani Toni. From here continue along the straight road, perhaps taking time to explore the church or to visit the old windmill (along a short track on the right at the far end of the village). The lighthouse at La Mola (➤ 22) and the welcome Es Puig bar are reached at 19km.

Return along the same (but much easier) route.

Where To...

Eivissa

Prices
Prices are approximate, based on a three-course meal for one, without wine but including coffee, in Eivissa:

£ = up to 1,800 psta
££ = 1,800–3,000 psta
£££ = over 3,000 psta

Mayonnaise
Mahón, the capital of the neighbouring island of Menorca, is famous for having given the world mayonnaise, a creation of the French's army's senior chef in 1756 after the French had ousted the British from the island.

Alfredo's (££)
Ibiza's oldest restaurant (though only dating from 1934), decorated with photos of the island before the tourist boom. Specialises in Spanish and Ibizan cooking. The mixed grills of fish and meat are a revelation, and the speciality 'black rice', made with sepia, is both exotic and delicious.
✉ 16 Paseo Vara de Rey
☎ 31 12 74 🕓 Lunch & dinner

Can des Parra (££)
Where many of Eivissa's residents eat – always the best of recommendations. Straightforward menu, but excellent service and cooking.
✉ 3 San Rafael ☎ 30 59 31
🕓 Lunch & dinner

Casino de Ibiza Restaurant (£££)
Very exclusive and expensive, but real quality. Passport needed for entry as it is inside the casino. This is *the* place to eat in Eivissa.
✉ The Casino, Paseo Juan Carlos ☎ 31 33 12 🕓 Dinner

De Gouwe Haan (££)
Dutch and Indonesian cooking, with one of the longest menus on the island. If the exotic flavours of *loempia*, *rijstafel* or *bami goreng* are not to your fancy, try an outsize T-bone steak or an excellent schnitzel.
✉ Figueretes Beach
☎ 30 19 14 🕓 Dinner
🏠 Eivissa–Platja d'en Bossa

Delfin Verde (£)
Spanish and Italian cooking. Excellent fish dishes.
✉ 2 Carrer Garijo ☎ 31 02 15
🕓 Lunch & dinner

El Brasero (£)
German cooking in the heart of Sa Penya.
✉ 4 Carrer Barcelona
☎ 31 14 69 🕓 Dinner

El Corsario (££)
The most famous establishment on the island. Eat and drink where Onassis and Dali dined.
✉ 5 Poniente, Dalt Vila
☎ 30 12 48 🕓 Dinner

El Faro (£)
Fish and shellfish on an elegant terrace in the harbour. The grouper and swordfish are especially worthwhile.
✉ 4 Plaça Garijo ☎ 30 10 52
🕓 Lunch & dinner

El Olivo (£££)
Brilliant position and menu. Booking recommended.
✉ 8 Plaça de Vila, Dalt Vila
☎ 30 06 80 🕓 Lunch & dinner

El Portalon (£££)
Spanish cooking of the highest standard with prices to match.
✉ Plaça des Desemparats, Dalt Vila ☎ 30 08 52
🕓 Dinner

Es Moli d'Or (£)
The best coffee and pastry in town. The Viennese pastries and savoury croissants are a must, and the filled baguettes eliminate the need for a more formal lunch. The café is ideally sited for people-watching.
✉ 39 Avenida Isidor Macabich, overlooking the harbour 🕓 Open all day

Formentera (£)
One of the town's foremost restaurants for typical Ibizan cooking, with dishes gently

flavoured with herbs. Situated close to the entrance to Dalt Vila, and a short distance from the harbour.

✉ **Plaça de Sa Tertiúlia** ☎ 31 10 24 🕐 **Lunch & dinner**

La Brasa (£)
One of the most attractive restaurants in Eivissa with a beautiful garden. Unusual, but excellent, fish and meat dishes.

✉ **3 Congresso Agricola** ☎ 30 12 02 🕐 **Dinner**

La Oliva (£)
Mediterranean cooking in very pleasant surroundings.

✉ **2 Santa Cruz** ☎ 30 06 80 🕐 **Dinner**

Los Valencianos (£)
Arguably the best ice-cream parlours on the island, serving home-made concoctions.

✉ **In Emili Pou near the Corsairs Monument and in Avenida Isidor Macabich, by the harbour** 🕐 **Open all day**

Meson de Paco (££)
Wood-fired Spanish cooking in a very atmospheric setting.

✉ **17 Bartolome Rosello** 🕐 **Dinner, closed Wed**

Nanking (££)
Arguably the most elegant Chinese restaurant in Ibiza. Excellent.

✉ **8 Obispo Cardona** ☎ 30 22 98 🕐 **Dinner**

Pacha Ibiza (£££)
Beautiful surroundings and an excellent menu.

✉ **27 Avendia Ocho de Agosto** ☎ 31 09 59 🕐 **Dinner**

Pinoch/Pinoch II (£)
Side by side restaurants offering excellent value for money.

✉ **16 and 18 Mayor** 🕐 **Lunch & dinner**

Plaza del Sol (£)
Eat on a terrace above the harbour.

✉ **Plaça del Sol, Dalt Vila** ☎ 39 07 73 🕐 **Lunch & dinner** 🚌 **A short walk from Eivissa**

Principe (££)
A lovely little restaurant overlooking the seafront at Figueretes. Specialises in fish and shellfish (some available from the large aquarium). The *paella* and Basque-style halibut are superb.

✉ **Ramon Mutaner, Figueretes** ☎ 30 19 14 🕐 **Lunch & dinner** 🚌 **A short walk from Eivissa**

Quefa-Bistro (£)
Very pleasant little bar/café.

✉ **9 Carrer Cayetà Soler** ☎ 30 29 72 🕐 **Open all day**

Romagna Mia (££)
In the slightly unfashionable end of town, but the best Italian cooking for miles.

✉ **Carrer Ramon Muntaner** ☎ 30 59 42 🕐 **Dinner**

Sa Caldera (££)
Unusual fish dishes of the highest standard and desserts to match.

✉ **19 Obispo Huix** ☎ 30 64 16 🕐 **Dinner**

Sausalito (£)
Surprisingly cheap for the quality. Very highly recommended.

✉ **5 Plaça de Sa Riba** ☎ 31 01 66 🕐 **Dinner**

Garum
For a taste of almost authentic Carthage, the Hotel Hacienda (► 101) offers game birds (pigeon, partridge etc) with figs or dates, and even swordfish with garum, a thick sauce prepared from pounded fish guts. Apparently to the Romans it was a delicacy, though from the description it is no surprise that it is no longer made here – or anywhere else.

Breakfast
The residents of the Pine Islands enjoy a simple, light breakfast, usually just coffee with a bread roll or pastry. If you are lucky, the pastries will be *ensaimadas* (► 56).

Ibiza

Bottled Water
Pine Island Water is chiefly produced by desalination and so has a slightly salty taste. To accompany meals it is better to drink mineral water (*agua mineral*) either *con gas* (carbonated) or *sin gas* (uncarbonated).

Cala Boix
Cala Boix (£)
A shady building near a delightful cove. The menu is straightforward, but the cooking is excellent and the surroundings could hardly be bettered.
✉ Cala Boix ☎ 33 52 24 🕐 Lunch & dinner 🚌 Not on a bus route

Cala d'Hort
Es Boldado (££)
Reached by a stiff climb or a rough drive but worth the effort whichever way you go. Specialises in fresh fish and langostines.
✉ Cala d'Hort ☎ 908 83 88 27 🕐 Lunch & dinner 🚌 Not on a bus route

Cala Llonga
La Casita (£££)
A rustic setting with a large terrace and magnificent views. The food is very good too.
✉ Urbanización Valverde, Cala Llonga, near Santa Eulària ☎ 33 02 93 🕐 Dinner, open all year 🚌 Eivissa–Santa Eulària

Wild Asparagus (££)
International cooking, ranging from steak to curry. Dinners under lanterns beside a pool. The desserts are a speciality: try the almond gateau or the restaurant's own version of sherry trifle.
✉ Cala Llonga ☎ 33 15 67 🕐 Lunch on Sun only, otherwise dinner. Closed Mon 🚌 Eivissa–Cala Llonga

Cala Mastella
Tio Bigotis Chiringuito (£)
Surely the most romantic eating house on Ibiza? Fresh fish – caught that morning by the owner– served in a rustic setting beside the lapping sea. But book and come early.
✉ Cala Mastella 🕐 Lunch 🚌 Not on a bus route

Cala Vadella
Bistro Jardin Indanh (£££)
International cuisine in a stunning setting on the cliffs above the cove.
✉ Cala Vadella 🕐 Dinner only 🚌 Eivissa–Cala Vadella

La Noria (££)
Delightful restaurant with excellent food in a remodelled Spanish village that is now a holiday complex.
✉ Vadella Pueblo, a little way inland from Cala Vadella ☎ 80 82 98 🕐 Lunch & dinner 🚌 Eivissa–Cala Vadella

Cala Xarraca
Cala Xarraca (££)
Wonderfully sited on the beach in the most exquisite of coves. The view alone is worth the price of a meal. Straightforward menu, but excellent cooking.
✉ Cala Xarraca ☎ 33 33 65 🕐 Lunch & dinner 🚌 Eivissa–Portinatx

Es Canar
Mar Bella (£)
Housed in white cubes that could have been the ones which inspired Le Corbusier, close to the beach. Simple, but good menu.
✉ Es Canar 🕐 Lunch & dinner 🚌 Santa Eulària–Es Canar

New Wave (££)
Inside and outside seating and food from a huge charcoal barbecue. Steaks and chicken served with jacket potatoes and salad. No fuss, just good.

☒ Es Canar ⓓ Dinner
🚌 Santa Eulària–Es Canar

Es Cavallet
La Escollera (££)
Very rustic setting just off
the beach at Es Cavallet.
Good food and moderate
prices.
☒ Es Cavallet beach ☎ 30
17 70 ⓓ Lunch & dinner
🚌 Not on a bus route

Es Cubells
Los Pinos (Es Pins) (££)
Pleasant, elegant restaurant
– with a menu and cooking
to match – coolly set
beneath the pines of the
name.
☒ Es Cubells ☎ 80 04 86
ⓓ Lunch & dinner

Jesús
Bon !.loc (££)
A very pleasant bar-cum-
restaurant close to the
church. The terrace
overlooks the main road and
can be noisy and fume-filled
at the wrong time of day, but
the cooking is excellent and
easily compensates.
☒ On the main road through
Jesús ☎ 31 18 13 ⓓ Lunch,
Dinner 🚌 Eivissa–Santa
Eulària

Platja d'en Bossa
Insula Augusta (££)
Right on the beach, an
excellent lunch spot.
☒ Southern end of Platja d'en
Bossa ☎ 39 08 82 ⓓ Lunch
& dinner 🚌 Eivissa–Platja
d'en Bossa

Port des Torrent
Palms (£)
Excellent Indian restaurant.
☒ Port des Torrent
ⓓ Dinner only. Closed Sun
🚌 Sant Antoni–Port des
Torrent–Portinatx

Cas Mallorqui (££)
Situated at the road's end, at
the water's edge in a small
cove. Fantastic views. Fish
only menu, but mouth-
wateringly excellent.
☒ Portinatx ☎ 33 30 82
ⓓ Lunch & dinner
🚌 Eivissa–Portinatx

Sant Agustí
Sa Tasca (£££)
International nouvelle cuisine
in elegant surroundings.
☒ Sant Agustí, near Sant
Josep ☎ 80 00 75 ⓓ Dinner,
open all year. Closed Mon
🚌 Eivissa–Sant Antoni

Sant Antoni
Escandells (£)
Open 22 hours daily for
freshly made fat food, vast
ice-creams and a panoramic
view of the bay. One of the
places to be seen.
☒ 1 Ample, by the fountains
☎ 34 00 27 ⓓ Lunch
🚌 Eivissa–Sant Antoni

Es Siti (££)
Typical Spanish cooking in
pleasant surroundings.
☒ 11a Carrer Sant Antoni
☎ 34 00 29 ⓓ Lunch &
dinner 🚌 Eivissa–Sant Antoni

Mei Ling (££)
The best Chinese restaurant
in town. All the usual
favourites and some
interesting fish dishes based
on local crab and scampi.
Takeaway service.
☒ Carrer Sant Antoni ☎ 34
34 14 ⓓ Lunch & dinner
🚌 Eivissa–Sant Antoni

Paris (££)
Choose your fish from the
large aquarium, then enjoy it
as the basis of a quality
meal. Paellas, zarauelas and
calderetas are a speciality,

Squid Speciality
Local squid is served
either as calamares (deep-
fried), or cooked in its own
ink. But to try a real local
speciality, ask for squid
that has been cut into thin
strips, then sun-dried and
barbecue-grilled. This will
be served with fresh
lemon.

Tapas

Spain invented the *tapas* bar. *Tapa* means lid and derives from an ancient custom of giving a small snack with a drink, placed on a saucer set on the drink glass like a lid. Today *tapas* bars are everywhere. *Tapas* can be anything that is bite-sized – olives, shellfish, ham, cheese, mushrooms. But beware – the food can be very tempting and it is easy to spend more on them than on a reasonable meal, so check the price of *una porción* before you start.

but there are also excellent steak dishes.

⊠ 28 Progresso ☎ 34 00 18
🕐 Lunch & dinner
🚌 Eivissa–Sant Antoni

Rias Baixas (££)

Really excellent meals and speciality home-made desserts.

⊠ 4 Carrer d'Ignasi Riquer
☎ 34 04 80 🕐 Lunch & dinner 🚌 Eivissa–Sant Antoni

Sa Prensa (£)

Specialises in fresh fish. Good food at reasonable prices.

⊠ 6 General Prim ☎ 34 16 70
🕐 Lunch & dinner 🚌 Sant Antoni beach bus

Sol y Sambra (££)

Typical Ibizan 'peasant' cooking, which means good, wholesome food, served in wonderfully pleasant surroundings

⊠ Platja es Pouet, near Sant Antoni 🕐 Lunch & dinner
🚌 Sant Antoni beach bus

Tijuana (££)

Mexican and Tex-Mex food served in Aztec-decorated restaurant. A very lively place.

⊠ Carrer Alacant (head inland from the sea)
☎ 34 24 73 🕐 Lunch & dinner 🚌 Eivissa– Sant Antoni

Sant Carles
Peralta (£)

Beautifully positioned, with wholesome food if you can ignore the hunting trophies. Try the roast chicken or the *sole meunière*. The desserts are typically Ibizan.

⊠ Sant Carles ☎ 33 25 11
🕐 Lunch & dinner. 🚌 Santa Eulària–Es Figueral

Sant Josep
Destino Tapas Bar (£)

Arguably the best *tapas* on the island.

⊠ Carrer Talaia 🕐 Open all day 🚌 Eivissa–Sant Antoni

Ruta (££)

Overlooking the church. Pleasant terrace and straight-forward, but excellent, menu.

⊠ Sant Josep ☎ 80 05 44
🕐 Lunch & dinner
🚌 Eivissa– Sant Antoni

Sant Miquel
Cafeteria Es Pi Ver (£)

Interesting café serving everything from squid in butter and *bullit de peix* to sausage, eggs and beans, and hamburger and chips.

⊠ Sant Miquel ☎ 80 82 98
🕐 Lunch & dinner
🚌 Eivissa– Portinatx

Sant Miquel (£)

Excellent pizzeria/restaurant with a bar/terrace.

⊠ Sant Miquel ☎ 33 25 67
🕐 Lunch & dinner
🚌 Eivissa– Portinatx

Sant Rafel
El Clodenis (££)

Provençale cooking at the heart of Ibiza.

⊠ Junto a la Iglesia ☎ 19 85 45 🕐 Dinner 🚌 Eivissa– Sant Rafel–Sant Antoni

L'Éléphant (£££)

Marvellous position and interesting external murals, but erratic cooking and service. Very good when it is good.

⊠ Plaça de la Iglesia ☎ 19 80 56/19 83 54 🕐 Dinner only 🚌 Eivissa–Sant Rafel

La Luna de Miel (££)

Half of one building, serving quality Vietnamese cooking.

✉ Sant Rafel ☎ 19 83 35
🕐 Dinner only 🚌 Eivissa–
Sant Rafel–Sant Antoni

La Luna de Miel (£)
The other half of the
building, a small *crêperie*.
✉ Sant Rafel ☎ 19 81 27
🕐 Lunch & dinner
🚌 Eivissa–Sant Rafel

Santa Eulària
Bahia (££)
Typical Ibizan cooking, but
more emphasis on meat
than fish. The shoulder of
lamb and pepper steak
brings clients back often,
while the *paella* is just as
good, as are the salads.
✉ On the seafront ☎ 33 08
28 🕐 Lunch & dinner
🚌 Eivissa–Santa Eulària

Delicias de Chine (££)
As delightful as the name.
Standard Chinese menu, but
served with elegance. Good
children's menu.
✉ 38 San Juan, overlooking
the harbour ☎ 33 93 41
🕐 Lunch & dinner
🚌 Eivissa–Santa Eulària

Doña Margarita (£££)
Overlooking the harbour.
One of the best restaurants
on the island with superb
fish and meat dishes.
✉ In the harbour ☎ 33 06 55
🕐 Lunch & dinner
🚌 Eivissa–Santa Eulària

La Posada (££)
Palm-fringed white cubes
below Puig de Missa.
Excellent.
✉ Puig de Missa 🕐 Lunch &
dinner 🚌 Eivissa–Santa
Eulària

Los Amigos (£)
Specialist *tapas* bar; arguably
the best in town.

✉ 28 Carrer Sant Vicent
🕐 Lunch & dinner
🚌 Eivissa– Santa Eulària

Pizzeria Magu (£)
Establishment with the best
view in town, right on Santa
Eulària's beautiful seafront.
Good pizzas, pasta and meat
dishes too.
✉ At the harbour end of the
seafront ☎ 33 93 26
🕐 Lunch & dinner
🚌 Eivissa–Santa Eulària

Rincon de Pepe (£)
A combination of a good
tapas bar and restaurant.
✉ 53 Carrer Sant Vicent
☎ 33 13 21 🕐 Lunch &
dinner 🚌 Eivissa–Santa
Eulària

The Steak and Cake (£)
Excellent place for families.
Covered terrace overlooking
the sea and everything from
pizza to curry.
✉ On the seafront 🕐 Open
all day 🚌 Eivissa–Santa
Eulària

Santa Gertrudis
Bar Costa (£)
One of the most famous
bars on Ibiza.
✉ Plaça de la Iglesia ☎ 19
70 21 🕐 Open all day 🚌 Not
on a bus route

La Plaza (£££)
French cuisine in a superb
garden setting.
✉ Plaça de la Iglesia ☎ 19
70 75 🕐 Dinner 🚌 Not on a
bus route

Santa Agnés
La Palmera (£)
Quiet little spot opposite the
church. Nothing fancy, but
delightful.
✉ Santa Agnés 🕐 Lunch &
dinner 🚌 Not on a bus route

Beach Food
For romance, as well as
convenience, the beach
restaurants are hard to
beat. Local regulations
require them to be
dismantled at the end of
each season, accounting
for the somewhat
ramshackle appearance of
some of them. Don't be
put off: the food will be
excellent, and the fish
could hardly be fresher.

Formentera

Sherry
Although not made here, sherry can be bought on the Pine Islands. The name derives from Jerez, where the original wine fortified with brandy was made. There are two types: *Fino* is a pale, dry apertif (*amontillado*, the most famous sherry, is a fino), while *oloroso* is a dark, sweet after-dinner drink.

Cala Saona
Es Pla (£)
Typical Island cooking in a pleasant garden. The position means that customers are usually the locals, so the authentic flavour of Formenteran cooking is preserved.
⊠ **Near the turn off to Cala Saona from the Sant Françesc–Cap de Barbaría road** ☎ **32 27 09** 🕔 **Lunch & dinner** 🚍 **Sant Françesc–Cala Saona**

Sol (££)
Fish dishes in beautiful surroundings, just a few steps from the beach.
⊠ **Cala Saona** ☎ **32 29 11** 🕔 **Lunch & dinner** 🚍 **Sant Françesc–Cala Saona**

Es Caló
Pep Paradis (££)
More than just a restaurant, as there is a swimming pool and apartments for hire. Enjoy the fine position overlooking the sea, as you try pizza, pasta and Italian meat dishes, or the fresh fish dishes which combine the best of both Spanish and Italian cooking.
⊠ **Es Caló** ☎ **32 72 32** 🕔 **Lunch & dinner** 🚍 **Sant Françesc–La Mola**

Es Pujols
Caminito (££)
An Argentinian steak house close to the beach. To find the restaurant, look for the cut-out tango-dancing figures!
⊠ **Es Pujols** ☎ **32 81 06** 🕔 **Dinner** 🚍 **Sant Françesc–Es Pujols**

Chez Fred (£)
Do not be put off by the name; this is a fine place,
with pizzas and some surprising international dishes.
⊠ **Es Pujols** ☎ **32 80 95** 🕔 **Lunch & dinner** 🚍 **Sant Françesc–Es Pujols**

El Paradiso (££)
Good quality Spanish and international cooking in pleasant surroundings.
⊠ **On the road from San Fernando (Sant Ferran) to Es Pujols** 🕔 **Lunch & dinner** 🚍 **Sant Françesc de Formentera–Es Pujols**

Le Cyrano (£££)
French cuisine of the highest standard. Try the house speciality *foie gras*, and remember that *caracoles abuela* are escargots.
⊠ **Avenida del Mar** ☎ **32 83 86** 🕔 **Lunch** 🚍 **Sant Françesc–Es Pujols**

Maritim (£)
From the name you could be forgiven for thinking that this was another fish restaurant. In fact it is an excellent pizzeria and ice-cream parlour. In the early morning it also sells excellent croissants.
⊠ **On the sea front, Es Pujols** 🕔 **Lunch & dinner** 🚍 **Sant Françesc–Es Pujols**

La Mola
El Mirador (£)
Without doubt the best view on the island, with all but the La Mola headland in view. The meat and fish dishes are excellent, but the *paella* demands a special mention.
⊠ **At the 14km post on Via Major from Sant Françesc to La Mola** ☎ **32 70 37** 🕔 **Lunch & dinner** 🚍 **Sant Françesc–La Mola**

La Savina
El Bergantin (££)
Paella, fish and meat – a standard menu, but good.

✉ **On the harbour front** ☎ **32 08 59** 🕐 **Lunch & dinner**

Nuevo Bellavista (££)
Typical island cuisine, with both meat and fish dishes. Close to the sea; the accent is on fish: the langostines are exceptional. Also very good is the typical *ensaladas payesas*.

✉ **La Savina** 🕐 **Lunch & dinner** ☎ **32 22 55/32 22 36**

Platja de Migjorn
Babarroja (£)
Freshly caught fish and typical island dishes. Try the *guisado de pescado* and the *arroz la marinera* for a real taste of Formentera. Beach terrace and swimming pool for those making rather more than just a meal of it.

✉ **Platja de Migjorn** ☎ **32 81 05** 🕐 **Lunch & dinner** 🚌 **Sant Françesc–Platja de Migjorn**

Es Codol Foradat (££)
One of the most varied of local menus, with both meat and fish dishes.

✉ **Platja de Migjorn** ☎ **32 82 81** 🕐 **Lunch & dinner** 🚌 **Sant Françesc–Platja de Migjorn**

Grill La Mola (£)
One of the best restaurants on the island, specialising in fresh fish and shellfish. The typical island dishes are the best items on an appealing menu.

✉ **Platja es Arenals, at the eastern end of Platja de Migjorn** ☎ **32 81 12** 🕐 **Lunch & dinner** 🚌 **Sant Françesc–Platja de Migjorn**

La Fragata (£)
Fresh fish and langostines within sight of the beach.

✉ **Platja de Migjorn** ☎ **908 73 27 47** 🕐 **Lunch & dinner** 🚌 **Sant Françesc–Platja de Migjorn**

Sant Ferran
Fonda Pepe (££)
Paella and other local dishes. The speciality *arroz la marinera* is definitely worth a try.

✉ **Sant Ferran** ☎ **32 80 33** 🕐 **Lunch & dinner** 🚌 **Sant Françesc–Es Pujols**

La Masia (££)
Catering for its own apartments, but also open to visitors, the restaurant has an excellent Indonesian menu. A remarkable find on the most unspoilt of all the Balearic islands.

✉ **Can Gavino** ☎ **32 24 21** 🕐 **Dinner** 🚌 **La Savina–Sant Françesc**

Sant Françesc
Can Gavino (££)
Quality international cuisine at reasonable prices.

✉ **Can Gavino** ☎ **32 24 21** 🕐 **Dinner** 🚌 **La Savina–Sant Françesc**

Casa Rafael (£)
Plain cooking, but excellent; where the locals eat.

✉ **Carrer d'Isidor Macabich** 🕐 **Lunch & dinner** 🚌 **La Savina–Sant Françesc**

Ses Illetes
Es Moli de Sal (££)
Romantically set in an old windmill above Ses Illetes beach. The food is good too.

✉ **Ses Illetes beach – follow the rough track** ☎ **908 13 67 73** 🕐 **Lunch & dinner** 🚌 **Not on a bus route**

The *Porrón*
The traditional Balearic wine-drinking vessel, with its wide body and tapered spout, looks like nothing so much as a miniature watering can. The locals make using them look easy, though visitors will discover that it takes several drenchings before any skill is achieved. Because no part of the *porrón* touches the drinker's mouth the vessel is very hygienic when passed around a group of workers or revellers, but legend has it that this was not the intent: the design was to allow the Moors to obey Islamic law that wine should not touch their lips!

Eivissa

Prices
Based on a standard double room in Eivissa:
£ = up to 6,000 psta
££ = 6,000–15,000 psta
£££ = over 15,000 psta

Favourite Haunt
Looking up at Dalt Vila from Eivissa's harbour, it is difficult to miss El Corsario, one of the island's most famous hotels and frequented by the rich and famous. Aristotle Onassis liked to sit on its terrace when his boat was moored in the harbour, and Salvador Dali stayed often.

Benjamin (£)
Small and neat, with good personal service, but limited facilities.
✉ Platja Talamanca ☎ 31 23 13 ⏰ Open Apr–Oct

Don Quijote (£)
Irresistible name. Limited facilities, but very pleasant.
✉ 10 Carrer Álava ☎ 30 18 69 ⏰ Open Apr–Oct

El Corsario (££)
One of the most famous hotels on Ibiza, with a fabulous position in Dalt Vila. Reasonable facilities.
✉ 5 Poniente, Dalt Vila ☎ 39 32 12 ⏰ Open all year

El Corso (££)
Not to be confused with the El Corsario. Large and with good facilities close to one of Eivissa's best beaches.
✉ Platja Talamanca ☎ 31 23 12 ⏰ Open Apr–Oct 🚌 Not on a bus route, but served by ferry from Eivissa harbour

Ibiza Platja (££)
Good facilities with the beach just moments away.
✉ Platja de Figueretes ☎ 30 28 04 ⏰ Open Apr–Oct

Isla (£)
Small and neat with limited facilities; close to the beach.
✉ Platja Talamanca ☎ 31 34 69 ⏰ Open Apr–Oct 🚌 Not on a bus route, but served by ferry from Eivissa harbour

Jabeque (££)
Large, but not impersonal. Good facilities.
✉ Carrer Carlos Román ☎ 30 41 11 ⏰ Open May–Oct

Los Molinos (£££)
Situated away from the city centre, but within 10 minutes' walk (and stiff climb) of Dalt Vila.
✉ 60 Carrer Ramon Muntaner ☎ 30 22 50 ⏰ Open all year 🚌 Not on a bus route

Mare Nostrum (££)
Very large, but welcoming. Good facilities.
✉ Avenida Pedro Matutes Noguera ☎ 30 26 62 ⏰ Open Apr–Oct

Montesol (£)
As close to the heart of the town as it is possible to get. Limited facilities.
✉ Paseo Vara de Rey ☎ 31 01 61 ⏰ Open all year

Platja Real (££)
Large hotel with good facilities on Eivissa's northern beach.
✉ 18 Ses Feixes, Talamanca ☎ 31 21 12 ⏰ Open May–Oct 🚌 Eivissa–Cap Martinet

Royal Plaza (£££)
Close to the centre of town. Listed as not having a restaurant, but it does – a good one. Excellent facilities including a roof-top swimming pool.
✉ 27–29 Carrer Pedro Francés ☎ 31 37 11 ⏰ Open all year

Torre del Mar (£££)
Aptly named large hotel close to the beach. All the facilities that anyone could wish for.
✉ Platja d'en Bossa ☎ 30 30 50 ⏰ Open Apr–Oct 🚌 Bus and ferry routes from Eivissa

Victoria (£)
Large, but pleasant. Reasonable facilities.
✉ Platja Talamanca ☎ 31 19 12 ⏰ Open Apr–Oct 🚌 Not on a bus route, but served by ferry from Eivissa harbour

Ibiza

Cala Llonga
Cala Llonga (££)
Reasonable facilities and close to the beach.
✉ Cala Llonga ☎ 33 08 87 🕐 Apr–Oct 🚌 Eivissa–Cala Llonga

Cala de Sant Vicenç
Imperio Platja (££)
Wonderfully situated in Cala Sant Vicenç. Excellent facilities.
✉ Cala de Sant Vicenç ☎ 33 30 55 🕐 Apr–Oct 🚌 Not on a bus route

Es Canar
Miami P (££)
Nicely positioned large hotel with good facilities.
✉ Platja Es Canar ☎ 33 02 01 🕐 May–Oct 🚌 Santa Eulària–Es Canar

Punta Arabí (£)
Small hotel, well situated and with good facilities.
✉ Punta Arabí, near Es Canar ☎ 33 01 52 🕐 Apr–Oct 🚌 Santa Eulària–Es Canar

Es Figueral
Club Cala Blanca (££)
On the beach at Es Figueral. Excellent facilities and a beautiful restaurant.
✉ Platja Es Figueral ☎ 33 51 00 🕐 May–Oct 🚌 Not on a bus route

Tennis (£)
Tiny, but very pleasant hotel. The game of the name is the only facility, but it is close to the beach.
✉ Platja Es Figueral ☎ 33 02 16 🕐 May–Oct 🚌 Not on a bus route

Platja d'en Bossa
Club Palm Beach (££)
Huge beach-side hotel with excellent facilities.
✉ Platja d'en Bossa ☎ 30 54 00 🕐 Apr–Oct 🚌 Eivissa–Platja d'en Bossa

Port des Torrent
Ibiza Pueblo (££)
Large hotel on the 'San Ant overflow' coast. Good facilities.
✉ Port des Torrent ☎ 34 05 12 🕐 Apr–Oct 🚌 Sant Antoni–Hotels of Port des Torrent

Portinatx
Cigüeña Platja
Small, beautifully sited hotel. Limited facilities, but the town and bay have everything most people could wish.
✉ Cala Portinatx ☎ 33 30 44 🕐 May–mid-Oct 🚌 Eivissa–Portinatx

Port de Sant Miquel
Club Cartago (££)
Futuristic building with excellent facilities and steps leading down to a beautiful cove.
✉ Puerto de Sant Miquel ☎ 33 45 51 🕐 Apr–Oct 🚌 Not on a bus route

Club Galeón (££)
Sister building to Club Cartago, and equally good.
✉ Port de Sant Miquel ☎ 33 45 34 🕐 Apr–Oct 🚌 Not on a bus route

Hacienda Na Xamena (£££)
Ibiza's most expensive and luxurious hotel. Everything you would expect from a 5-star establishment. Beautifully situated in a quiet, cliffside position.
✉ Near Port de Sant Miquel ☎ 33 45 00 🕐 Apr–Oct 🚌 Not on a bus route, but visitors to the Hacienda do not usually arrive by bus

Accommodation Classification
The Spanish classification for accommodation is quite complex. An establishment is classified as H (Hotel), HR (Hotel Residencia), HA (Hotel Apartamentos), RA (Residencia Apartamentos), M (Motel), Hs (Hostel), P (Pension) or HsR (Hostal Residencia). To reduce confusion, just remember that an R in the classification means there will *not* be a dining room (though the establishment may offer breakfast). The classification then runs from full-service hotels (H) to guest houses (P).

Winter Closing

If you are visiting the Pine Islands off-season be sure to check whether your chosen hotel will be open. Most of the island's hotels close from November to March or April, and some of those that do remain open only do so to cater for older folk who are on long-stay packages.

Sant Antoni

Mitjorn (£)

Small, but nicely situated between beach and harbour. Limited facilities.

✉ 6 Carrer del Faro ☎ 34 09 02 🕐 May–Oct

🚌 Eivissa–Sant Antoni

Nautilus (£££)

The most expensive hotel in Sant Antoni. Excellent facilities and a superb position.

✉ Bahia de Sant Antoni ☎ 34 04 00 🕐 Apr–Oct

🚌 Eivissa–Sant Antoni

Palmyra (££)

At the south end of town, close to a quieter beach. Good facilities.

✉ Avenida Dr Fleming ☎ 34 03 54 🕐 Apr–Oct

🚌 Eivissa–Sant Antoni

Tanit (££)

Close to the harbour. Excellent facilities.

✉ Cala Gracio ☎ 34 13 00 🕐 May–Oct 🚌 Eivissa–Sant Antoni

Vedra (£)

Small, neat hotel close to the harbour. Limited facilities.

✉ 7 Carrer del Mar ☎ 34 01 50 🕐 Apr–Oct 🚌 Eivissa-Sant Antoni

Tropical (££)

In the middle of the town. Reasonable facilities, but you need to travel to the beaches etc.

✉ Carrer Cervantes, ☎ 34 00 50 🕐 Apr–Oct 🚌 Eivissa-Sant Antoni

Santa Eulària

Buenavista (£)

The view of the name is of Puig de Missa and the southern end of the town. Limited facilities.

✉ Carrer Sant Jaime, near foot of Puig de Missa ☎ 33 00 03 🕐 Apr–Oct

La Cala (££)

Large hotel with reasonable facilities. Close to Puig de Missa and a good base for the eastern coast.

✉ 76 Carrer Sant Jaime ☎ 33 00 09 🕐 All year 🚌 Eivissa–Santa Eulària

Mediterráneo (£)

Very pleasant little hotel with surprisingly good facilities.

✉ 1 Carrer Pinto Vizcai ☎ 33 00 15 🕐 All May–Sep 🚌 Eivissa–Santa Eulària

San Marino (£££)

Santa Eulària's most expensive hotel. Excellent facilities.

✉ 1 Carrer Ricardo Curtoys Gotarredona ☎ 33 03 16 🕐 All year 🚌 Eivissa–Santa Eulària

Sol S'Argamassa (££)

Large but excellent hotel in a 'new' resort. Good facilities.

✉ S'Argamassa, near Santa Eulària ☎ 33 00 75 🕐 Apr–Oct 🚌 Santa Eulària–Es Canar

Tres Torres (££)

Situated on the harbour front. Excellent facilities.

✉ Puerto Deportivo ☎ 33 03 26 🕐 Apr–Oct 🚌 Eivissa–Santa Eulària

Santa Agnés

Don Juan (£)

Lovely little place in the middle of one of Ibiza's quietest areas. However, there is no restaurant and limited facilities.

✉ Santa Agnés ☎ 34 12 12 🕐 Apr–Oct 🚌 Not on a bus route

Formentera

Cala Saona
Cala Saona (£££)
Situated almost on the beach in this beautiful cove. Good facilities.

✉ Cala Saona ☎ 32 20 30 🕔 Apr–Oct 🚌 Sant Françesc–Cala Saona

El Pilar
Entrepinos (£)
Just about the only hotel on the La Mola plateau, but none the worse for that. Reasonable facilities including bicycle hire – and in the perfect position for guests to make use of them.

✉ El Pilar ☎ 32 70 17 🕔 May–Oct 🚌 Limited bus service in summer months

Es Pujols
Lago Platja (£)
Small, but with good facilities for its size and class. The restaurant specialises in German food.

✉ Platja de Sa Roqueta, to the north of Es Pujols ☎ 32 85 51 🕔 May–Oct 🚌 Not on a bus route

Los Rosales (£)
Small and neat. Limited facilities. Close to the centre of town and the beach.

✉ Near the centre of Es Pujols ☎ 32 81 23 🕔 Apr–Oct 🚌 Sant Françesc–Es Pujols

Rosamar (£)
Neat little hotel with pleasant restaurant. Limited facilities, but close to the town.

✉ Platja de Sa Roqueta, to the north of Es Pujols ☎ 32 81 98/32 84 73 🕔 May–Oct 🚌 Not on a bus route

Tahití (£)
Large, but modest. Very pleasant. Limited facilities.

✉ Platja de Es Pujols ☎ 32 81 22 🕔 Apr–Oct 🚌 Sant Françesc–Es Pujols

Voramar (£)
Beautiful little building with lovely galleries. Small, with limited facilities. The hotel advertises itself as being especially good for sangria – who could argue?

✉ Near the centre of Es Pujols ☎ 32 81 19 🕔 May–Oct 🚌 Sant Françesc–Es Pujols

La Savina
Bellavista (££)
Conveniently sited for travellers, not so good for a static stay. Good facilities.

✉ Plaça de la Marina ☎ 32 22 55 🕔 All year

Platja de Migjorn
Casbah Mitjorn (£)
An unlikely name, but a very pleasant little hotel with excellent facilities and close to the beach.

✉ Platja de Migjorn ☎ 32 20 51 🕔 May–Oct 🚌 Sant Françesc–Platja de Migjorn

Formentera (£££)
Situated on the beach. Good facilities.

✉ Platja de Migjorn ☎ 32 00 00 🕔 Apr–Oct 🚌 Sant Françesc–Platja de Migjorn

Riu Club la Mola (£££)
The most expensive hotel on the island, with all the facilities you would expect.

✉ Platja de Migjorn ☎ 32 80 69 🕔 May–Sep 🚌 Sant Françesc–Platja de Migjorn

Sant Françesc de Formentera
La Savina (£)
✉ 22 Avenida Mediterránea ☎ 32 22 79 🕔 Mid-Apr–Sep 🚌 Sant Françesc–Platja de Migjorn

Camping
Camping is not permitted on Formentera, but there are several sites on Ibiza – three near Sant Antoni and two on the coast near Santa Eulária.

Shopping Ideas

Exchange Rates

If you can use a Visa or Mastercard, then it is probably worthwhile, as the rate of exchange the major credit card companies offer is better than the tourist rate. If not, use pesetas, as the rates most shops offer for dollars or pounds sterling are poor in comparison to those of big exchange bureaux.

Fashion

About 25 years ago a specific form of fashion grew up in Ibiza. Known as Ad Lib, the fashion – though evolving as it must – has withstood the test of time and has even influenced world-wide fashion. The shops selling Ad Lib on Ibiza come and go frequently as young designers move in for a season or two and then move on.

Below are some of the more important fashion outlets which seem to be more permanent. Some of these would frown at being called Ad Lib, but are up-to-the-minute and well worth a look.

'Official' Ad Lib

Antonio Siligato
A Florentine jewellery-maker.
✉ 15B Carrer Cataluña, Eivissa

Arrebato
Created in 1984 by Enrique Paege García. The definitive Ad Lib interior design and decoration company, responsible for the design of several of Ibiza's discos.
✉ Apdo 153, Es Canar ☎ 33 23 96

Artesania Urbana
Highly original fashion for the young set.
✉ 1 Sant Jaime, Santa Eulària ☎ 33 24 67

B&M Pell
Leatherwork – sharing an outlet with Romero.
✉ 32 Carrer Atzaró, Eivissa ☎ 30 45 80

Capricci
Young, high-quality fashion.
✉ 8 Avenida Ignacio Wallis, Eivissa ☎ 31 42 56

Catalina Bonet
High-class fashion that is frequently seen in the Madrid shows.
✉ 1 Paseo Juan Carlos, Eivissa ☎ 31 28 63

Chapeau Ibiza
With all that sun a hat is a must. And at night it is even more of a must. Ibiza's only local-made hat shop.
✉ Can Benet, Sant Rafel ☎ 19 80 89

Charo Ruiz
Simplicity and elegance, with a terrific use of colour.
✉ 34 Centra Aeropuerto, Eivissa ☎ 39 66 96

Dalias
One of the most distinctive outlets in the centre of 'young Ibiza'.
✉ 38 Carrer del Mar, Sant Antoni ☎ 19 01 20

Dario Bomé
Fine leatherwork on the road to the church in Sant Miguel.
✉ 10 Carrer Iglesia, Sant Miguel ☎ 33 48 33

Diseño y Moda
Particularly noted for clever use of colour.
✉ 127 Carrer Cataluña, Eivissa ☎ 39 15 75

Jazz Taller Pieles
Smart leather and suede fashion.
✉ 34 Calle de la Virgen, Eivissa ☎ 31 65 22

Jess i Joy
Two outlets for male and female fashion.
✉ 18 Calle de la Cruz, Eivissa ☎ 19 13 70

Jose y Julia
Interesting thoughts on shoe and sandal design.
✉ 337 Maestro Artesano, Xomeu Mayans, Sant Ferran, Formentera ☎ 32 63 12

Mapa Mundi
Fashion including both modern and older fabrics.
✉ 13A Plaça de Vila Dalt, Eivissa ☎ 39 16 85

Maria M
Very up-market label, with clients throughout the world. Most designs are in cotton.
✉ 2 Calle Rimbau, Eivissa ☎ 31 08 61

Marta Raffo
A variety of fabrics and some outrageous ideas which have caught the eye in shows as far away as Tokyo.
✉ 63 Calle de la Girgen, Eivissa ☎ 31 84 42

Maru Garcia
One of the pioneers of Ad Lib and still one of the top names. Shares an address with the interior designer Arrebato.
✉ Apdo 153, Es Canar ☎ 33 23 96

Perlotti and Giannini
Clever use of patchwork and other unusual ideas.
✉ 12 Via Púnica, Eivissa ☎ 30 25 68

Romero
Leather belts and sandals, also interesting craftwork.
✉ 32 Carrer Atzaró, Eivissa ☎ 30 45 80

Salambo
The outlet name of Cristina Buscetto, a designer of high quality Ad Lib for almost 20 years.
✉ 4 Calle José Verdera ☎ 39 08 54

TomTom
Elegant designs from a long-standing Ad Lib design team.
✉ 43B Carrer Progresso ☎ 39 16 85

Triana
Fine leatherwork, specialising in handbags.
✉ Lista de Correos, Santa Eulària ☎ 33 48 33

'Unofficial' Outlets

Bianca
The definitive Ad Lib outlet.
✉ 37 Calle de la Virgen

Flower Power
Hippy power is alive and well and even looking modern.
✉ Calle Montgrí

Joy Borne
Ladies' fashions.
✉ Calle José Verdera ☎ 31 09 72

Lipstik
Ladies' fashions in cool materials and colours.
✉ 22–24 Carrer Pedro Francés ☎ 31 54 60

Paula's
'Of-the-moment' Ibizan styles.
✉ 4 Carrer de la Virgen ☎ 31 61 91

Antiques and Objets d'Art

Casi Casa
Gifts and *objets d'art*.
✉ 5 Paseo Vara de Rey, Eivissa ☎ 39 10 00

El Palio and Siena
A pair of shops separated by a more business-like establishment. Pottery,

Public Holidays

Spain has the following national public holidays:

1 January
6 January
19 March
Maundy Thursday
Good Friday
Easter Monday
1 May
24 June
25 July
15 August
12 October
1 November
Immaculate Conception (usually 8 December)
25 December

In addition to the above, there are frequent saints' days when the shops throughout Ibiza and/or Formentera, or in individual towns and villages, will close.

antiques and *objets d'art*.
✉ **Near Plaça de la Iglesia, Santa Gertrudis**

Galleria Can Daifa

A delightful little shop with a fountain in its courtyard. Sells paintings, mirrors and pottery.
✉ **Near Plaça de la Iglesia, Santa Gertrudis**

Te Quiera

Curios and unusual gift ideas.
✉ **7 Carrer Castilla, Eivissa**
☎ **39 06 95**

Timor Gallery

Art and antiques from North Africa, Asia and South America as well as from mainland Spain and the island.
✉ **On the main road between Eivissa and Santa Eulària**
☎ **33 93 21** 🚉 **Eivissa–Santa Eulària**

Vivian Scott

One of Ibiza's foremost antiques shops.
✉ **1 Calle Jaume, Eivissa**

Paintings and Sculpture

Asociación Wendy Williams

An association of local artists specialising particularly in mosaics.
✉ **Apartado 7, Sant Josep**
☎ **80 01 38**

Buddhas

A painting gallery which also operates as a bar and restaurant.
✉ **On the C733 Eivissa–Portinatx road, close to the bridge over the Rio Santa Eulària, near the turn off to Santa Eulària and Sant Rafel**

Galleria Carl van de Voort

Paintings – one of the leading Ibizan galleries.
✉ **13 Plaça de la Vila, Dalt Vila, Eivissa** ☎ **30 06 49**

Galleria Lanz

Paintings, sculptures and pottery.
✉ **Plaça de Vila, Dalt Vila, Eivissa**

Libro Azul

International book shop and art gallery.
✉ **Urbacion Sa Nova Gertrudis, Santa Gertrudis**
☎ **19 74 54**

Michelangelo's

Pottery, paintings on wood and jewellery.
✉ **Near Baluarte Puerto Nueva, Dalt Vila, Eivissa**

Timor Gallery

Art and antiques from north Africa, Asia and South America as well as from mainland Spain and the island itself.
✉ **On the main road between Eivissa and Santa Eulària, soon after that road branches off the C733 Eivissa to Portinatx road**
☎ **33 93 21** 🚉 **Eivissa–Santa Eulària**

Ceramics and Pottery

Art and Joy

Local pottery and an interesting selection of unusual gifts.
✉ **19 Carrer del Mar, La Marina, Eivissa** ☎ **31 79 13**

Artesana El Paraiso

Gold and silver-plated ceramics and Mallorca pearls. This is also the official stockist of Lladro and Nao.

Carrer del Mar, Santa Eulària

Ca Vostra
A range of locally made pottery.

Carrer Esconellas, Sant Josep ☎ 34 14 21

Cerámicas
Pottery including 'authorised' Punic reproductions.

Corner of Carrer d'Arago & L'Historiador Josef Clapés, Eivissa

Cerámicas Icardi
Craft pottery made by Carlos Icardi Martinez. Wonderful work.

Can Ferreret, Sant Rafel ☎ 19 81 06

Cerámicas Kinoto
Another master craftsman's work.

Can Kinoto, Sant Rafel ☎ 19 82 62

Dom
An interesting range of porcelain and various glass gifts.

7 Carrer de la Creu, Sa Penya, Eivissa ☎ 19 01 68

El Moham
Locally made pottery and general gifts.

Plaça de la Vila, Dalt Vila, Eivissa ☎ 30 05 10

Es Moli
Excellent work from a collection of local craft potters.

Escuelas Viejas, Sant Rafel ☎ 19 81 36

Es Pins
A selection of pottery and plants.

On the road to Cala Saona, Formentera

Maribiza
An interesting range of hand-painted pottery.

72 Calle de la Virgen, Eivissa

Michelangelo's
Pottery, paintings on wood and jewellery.

Near Baluarte Puerta Nueva, Dalt Vila, Eivissa

Turren Fon-Du
Ceramics, leather and toys, some made on the premises. Includes reproduction antiques and genuine Ibizenco crafts upstairs, while on the ground floor there is a large toyshop and leatherware.

On the steps beside the Post Office, Santa Eulària

Clothing and Shoes

Atlantis Boutique
Come here to buy T-shirts and a range of ladies' and men's fashions.

Es Pujols, Formentera ☎ 32 82 41

Boutique Babalu
Eccentric fashions for the young.

Carrer d'Isidor Macabich, Sant Françesc de Formentera

Boutique Winnie
Ladies' fashions made by Winnie herself, together with straw hats and attractive accessories, such as hand-made jewellery.

In the pedestrian walkway, Sant Carles

Hibisco
A combined boutique and perfumery.

Avenida Miramar, Es Pujols, Formentera ☎ 32 82 32

Early Days

When postal services began on Ibiza the mail was brought by ship from Palma de Mallorca each morning, return mail being taken away by the same ship each evening. From Eivissa the postman walked to Sant Antoni and Santa Eulària, returning the same evening with the outgoing mail. As soon as someone pointed out that it would be quicker if the postman had a horse, one was bought. However, it was soon realised that though this speeded up the postman on Ibiza, the mail service was still dependent on the speed of the boat, so the horse was sold. The feelings of the postman are not recorded.

Magic Shoes
The latest offerings in fashion shoes.
✉ **2 Paseo Vara de Rey**

Sandal Shop
The best leather sandals on the island. Made to measure sandals completed in time to wear for the last part of your holiday.
✉ **2 Plaça de la Vila, Dalt Vila, Eivissa** ☎ **30 54 75**

Embroidery

Bernat Vinya
A bar/café (on the route of the walk to Ibiza's highest point ► 53) that also stocks a range of locally made embroidery.
✉ **Plaça de la Iglesia, Sant Josep** ☎ **34 07 03**

Hippy Markets

One of the great joys of the Pine Islands are the hippy markets. Originally these really were full of stalls owned by hippies selling their own work. Today they are outlets for craft workers selling everything from toys to clothes.

At the hippy markets it is perfectly acceptable to haggle over prices. At other street markets haggling may also be worth a try, but be careful: Ibiza is not a third world country where visitors with cash can barter prices down. The prices shown in shops and many markets are real, just as they are at home, and the trader may be annoyed if you expect to pay less.

Club Punta Arabí
The original hippy-run market.

✉ **Es Canar** ◷ **Wed 9–7**

Las Dalias
El Mercado de las Cosas Buenos (The Market of Good Things) – arts, crafts, clothes.
✉ **At the 12km post on the main road near Sant Carles** ☎ **33 50 42** ◷ **Sat 9–7**

Platja d'en Bossa
◷ **Fri 11–8**

Formentera
Es Pujols
◷ **Daily 6–10**

Sant Françesc
◷ **Daily 9–2**

El Pilar
◷ **Sun 4–9**

Jewellery

Antonio Siligato
Ad Lib jewellery by an Italian designer.
✉ **15B Carrer Cataluña, Eivissa** ☎ **39 08 54**

Joyeria Guillem
Watches and jewellery, the latter including some beautiful hand-painted gemstones and Ibizenco wedding jewellery.
✉ **9 Calle Vicente Cuervo, Eivissa** ☎ **31 17 76**

Knitwear

Mercería La Mola
Locally produced knitwear items.
✉ **El Pilar, Formentera**

Leather

B&M Pell
Ad Lib Leatherwork - sharing an outlet with Romero
✉ **32 Carrer Atzaró, Eivissa** ☎ **30 45 80**

Cas Sabater
A craft leather-worker based in one of the most delightful and out-of-the-way villages on Ibiza. Shoes made to measure.
✉ **Santa Agnés**

Cuero
✉ **Plaça de la Iglesia, Santa Gertrudis**

Dario Bomè
✉ **10 Carrer Iglesia (the road to the church), Sant Miquel**
☎ **33 33 96**

Luis Gercowski
Exciting work from a brilliant craftsman.
✉ **3 Can Sango, Santa Eulària**

Ricardo Lucio Moreira
Another brilliant craftsman selling his wares.
✉ **Apartado 344, Sant Antoni**
☎ **34 28 49**

Romero
Romero sells leather belts and other accessories, as well as some interesting craftwork.
✉ **32 Carrer Artzaró, Eivissa**
☎ **30 45 80**

Triana
Fine leatherwork, in an outlet that specialises mainly in handbags.
✉ **Lista de Correos, Santa Eulària** ☎ **333 48 33**

Musical Instruments

Can Vicenç des Ferrer
Musical instruments could provide souvenir ideas: come here for traditional Formenteran instruments.
✉ **Sant Françesc de Formentera**

Francesc Bufí
Traditional Ibizan instruments.
✉ **Sa Tenquete, Jesús**

Yaron Percusión
Traditional Ibizan instruments, but specialising in percussion.
✉ **Apartado 177, Sant Antoni**
☎ **34 31 44**

Perfume
All the main towns have perfumeries selling (or claiming to sell) named perfumes at duty free prices. Be cautious and shop around before buying, however, as not all the prices are as low as they seem.

One genuinely low-priced outlet is Groch, which also offers some Spanish and Ibizan fragrances which tend to be difficult to obtain elsewhere.
✉ **On the main road through Es Canar**

Wine and Spirits
As is the case with the perfumeries, there are many wine and spirits outlets claiming to sell their products at duty free prices. Again, you should be cautious when making any purchase.

There are also many outlets selling local *hierbas*, though not all offer a full range. To see that, try:

Bodegas Ribas
A full range of Ibizan *hierbas*, together with a vast choice of Spanish (as well as French and other) wines and spirits from all over the world. Tax free and special offers are available.
✉ **Carrer Sant Vicent, Santa Eulària**

Common Sense
The Pine Islands are no more hazardous for the visitor than any other part of Europe. Indeed, away from the towns and beaches they are far more peaceable. However, it pays to take the usual precautions: be careful with your valuables, particularly on the beach and in crowded market and shop areas where pickpockets thrive, and do not leave articles on show in your car.

Children in Ibiza & Formentera

Public Toilets
These are in very, very short supply on Ibiza and Formentera, which can make travelling with children a problem. However, most bars will allow you to use their toilets – though buying a cup of coffee is a good way of ensuring co-operation.

Amusement Park
Behind the Panorama Hotel in Es Canar there is a mini-amusement park with trampolines, rides, pool tables and arcade games.

Cycling and Mountain Biking
The roads of Ibiza are a little too dangerous for inexperienced or young cyclists. However, both on Ibiza and Formentera there are green routes which can be explored on mountain bikes. On Ibiza a map is available from the Tourist office giving details of available routes – ask for *Rutas en Mountain Bike*. The map – in English, French, German and Italian as well as Spanish – also has details of specific itineraries near the larger towns (Eivissa, Sant Antoni and Santa Eulària). These itineraries even include a cross-section of the route so that cyclists can see the extent of climbing.

On Formentera a pamphlet is produced giving details of Green Tours (the name of the pamphlet). The pamphlet includes details of 10 cycle/mountain bike itineraries, together with a further nine walking routes.

All of the islands' cycle-hire shops stock mountain bikes as well as road cycles, and most also have crash helmets for hire.

Glass-bottomed Boats
There are glass-bottomed boats at several of Ibiza's coves, most particularly at Sant Antoni and Port des Torrent. Ask at the Tourist Office for details.

Go-Karts
There is go-karting at: Eivissa, close to the airport, at Sant Antoni (☎ 34 38 05) and at Santa Eulària.

Horse Riding
Ibiza seems to have been made for exploration on horseback, with specific tracks having been created to explore the wilder parts of the island. Visitors of all ages looking for a gentle way of exploring the island's scenery should contact one of the following riding schools. At each of these, horses can be hired or children can join a trek. Treks can last from a couple of hours to a half-day or even longer if required.

Can Cirer
✉ On the road to Pike's Hotel, Sant Antoni
☎ 34 15 54

Can Dog
✉ On the road from Eivissa to Sant Joan, at the 14km post near Sant Llorenç
☎ 908 35 81 07

Easy Rider
✉ On the road to the campsite, Cala Llonga
☎ 19 65 11

Escuela de Equitacion Can Mayans
✉ Santa Gertrudis
☎ 908 63 68 84

Es Puig
✉ Finca Can Puig, Santa Gertrudis
☎ 19 71 66

Las Cuadras Ibiza
✉ On the old road from Eivissa to Jesús
☎ 19 70 11

Saona Horses
✉ C'an Jeroni, Sant Françesc de Formentera ☎ 32 30 01

Play Areas
All Ibiza's towns and larger villages have excellent play areas for younger children. These areas, well protected from roads and usually with a brightly painted mural, tend to be at the centre of the village.

Sailing
Sailing lessons for 10-15 year olds are available at:

Club Náutico de Ibiza
✉ Eivissa
☎ 31 33 63

Club Náutico de Sant Antoni
✉ Sant Antoni
☎ 34 06 45
🚌 Eivissa-Sant Antoni

Sports Centres
Indoor tennis, squash, badminton etc are available at the following centres:

El Polideportivo Municipal de Eivissa
✉ Can Misses, Eivissa
☎ 31 35 64

El Polideportivo Municipal de Sant Antoni de Portmany
✉ Sant Antoni
☎ 34 54 02

Tuition is available at these centres and the island also has possibilities for tuition in more specialist sports such as rowing and archery, or even in the use of the sling-shot, for which early Ibizans were famed (and feared). Ask at the Tourist

Information Offices for details of courses in your area.

Water Parks
There are two excellent water parks with pools and water slides on Ibiza:

Aqualandia
✉ Cap Martinet, Talamanca
☎ 19 24 111
🕐 Daily 10–7
🚌 Eivissa-Cap Martinet

Aguamar
✉ Platja d'en Bossa
☎ 39 67 90
🕐 Daily 10–7
🚌 Eivissa-Platja d'en Bossa

Water Sports
On many of the islands' beaches pedaloes, small surf boards and canoes are available for hire. Many of the beaches also now have 'sky buses' - inflated tubes on which children sit and are towed behind a motor boat. These rides are quite safe, though parents should be more careful with 'doughnutting', where the rider sits in an inflated inner tube and is towed behind a motor boat. Serious accidents have occurred in other countries with these rides. The worse that can happen on a sky bus is that the children will fall into the water – and that is part of the fun.

On most of Ibiza's beaches the swimming is excellent. Page 40 has a list of the best (ie safest) beaches on the islands for children. Please remember, however, that there are no lifeguards on any of the islands' beaches.

Local Events
At the local saint's day celebrations in towns and villages on Ibiza and Formentera there are usually events and entertainments arranged for children, and visitors are welcome to take part. If you are really lucky, the entertainment will include a greasy pole with a prize for anyone who can reach the top.

Entertainment & Sports

What's On

The local newspaper is the daily *Diario de Ibiza*, published in Catalan, but with a supplement in German during the summer months. This paper is particularly useful for its local information as it publishes the local bus and ferry timetables, the whereabouts of their pharmacies and their opening times, and the location of 24-hour petrol stations. It also includes weekly calendars of events.

There is also a weekly magazine/newspaper called *Ibiza Now*, published in English during the summer months.

Casino

Casino de Ibiza

The islands' only casino, with all the usual games. There is also a nightclub with a cabaret and a restaurant (one of the best on Ibiza). Entry by passport only.

✉ **Ibiza Marina, Eivissa**
☎ **31 33 12** 🕐 **10PM–5AM**

Discos

Ibiza is famous for its discos. Below is a list of the bigger, better known establishments. In general, the discos listed below are at their best after 1AM. If you are looking for something exotic, keep your eye on the local press or ask about at your resort. Ibiza is famous (infamous ?) for its disco nights specifically aimed at gay travellers or those seeking an outrageously good time. If you are interested in a transvestite evening, entering a beauty competition – topless for ladies, mini-thong for gents – then Ibiza's discos were built just for you. But even if something less decadent is more to your taste, a visit to one of the island's top discos is worth considering. The light shows alone make them worthwhile and they are ideal for people watching.

Amnèsia

Less flamboyant than Privilege (► below) and a good deal less frenetic, but still one of Ibiza's top two or three.

✉ **On the Sant Antoni to Eivissa road, at the 6km post**
☎ **19 80 41** 🕐 **10PM–9AM**

El Divino

Currently the 'in place' on Ibiza – but who knows what next year will bring.

✉ **Puerto Deportivo Nueva, Eivissa** ☎ **19 01 76**
🕐 **10PM–5AM**

Es Paradís

Definitely a venue for the young and those with stamina.

✉ **Sant Antoni** 🕐 **11PM–6AM**

Lola's

Claims to be Ibiza's oldest disco and could well be right. Smaller than the other famous venues and, as a consequence, a little more intimate.

✉ **9 Carrer Alfonso XII, Sa Penya, Eivissa** 🕐 **11PM–3AM**

Pacha

Famous for its parties. The fun includes indoor swimming pools. The restaurant is famed for its Basque cooking.

✉ **Paseo Mantimo, Eivissa**
☎ **31 09 59** 🕐 **8PM–6AM**

Privilege (KU)

Arguably the best disco in the world). Certainly one of the biggest with a capacity of thousands, an indoor pool and a restaurant. It is hard to miss – look for the space-age dome to your left just after you pass Sant Rafel on the road from Sant Antoni to Eivissa.

✉ **Sant Rafel** ☎ **19 81 60**
🕐 **8PM–6AM**

Space

Huge and with equally huge sound and light systems. An epic experience.

✉ **Platja d'en Bossa** ☎ **39 67 94** 🕐 **8PM–6AM**

Zulu (Angel's)

Formerly called Angel's but now known as Zulu, defintely

a disco for the younger set only.

✉ **Paseo Maritimo** ☎ 34 16 12 🕐 11PM–6AM

Diving

Ibiza and Formentera have some of the clearest waters in the Mediterranean, with visibility up to 40m. With summer water temperatures rising to 28°C this makes the islands an ideal place to dive or to learn to dive. Lucky divers may see sleeper lobsters, groupers, sunfish and perhaps even a school of barracuda. Everyone will see coral reefs. Making contact with a local club will allow you to learn the position of interesting wrecks and the whereabouts of underwater caves. All divers on Ibiza and Formentera have access to the decompression chamber at the La Sirena club in Sant Antoni.

The following clubs will help novices and experienced divers. All the clubs are affiliated to at least one of the world's major sub-aqua organisations.

Anfibios
✉ **Platja d'en Bossa** ☎ 19 24 18

Aqua-Nautic
✉ **Platja de Cala Vadella** ☎ 80 82 67

Cala Pada
✉ **Platja de Cala Pada, Santa Eulària** ☎ 33 07 55

Figueral
✉ **Platja des Figueral** ☎ 33 50 79

Free Delfin Diving
✉ **Hotel Club Delfin, Cala Codolar** ☎ 80 62 10

✉ **Hotel El Corso, Talamanca** ☎ 31 35 24

Ibiza Diving
✉ **Puerto Deportivo, Santa Eulària** ☎ 33 29 49

La Sirena
✉ **21 Carrer Balanzat, Sant Antoni** ☎ 34 29 66

Nemo
✉ **Club Punta Arabí, Es Canar** ☎ 33 15 15

Orca Sub
✉ **Club Hotel Cala Tarida Beach** ☎ 80 62 53

Rumbo Azul
✉ **Apartamento Montemar, Cala Llonga** ☎ 19 65 06

Sant Miquel
✉ **Port de Sant Miquel** ☎ 33 45 39

Sea Horse Club
✉ **Port des Torrent** ☎ 34 64 38

Subfari
✉ **Cala Portinatx** ☎ 33 31 83

Vellmarí
✉ **90 Avenida del Mediterráneo, La Savina, Formentera** ☎ 32 21 05

Golf

There is only one course on Ibiza, though there is at present a vigorous public debate over a proposal to construct another near Cala d'Hort.

El Club de Golf de Ibiza
✉ **On the road from Eivissa to Cala Llonga** ☎ 31 52 03

Horse-racing

Horse-racing and trotting races can be seen at two venues. During the summer

Two Wheels

More convenient than a car for parking – though more dangerous on Ibiza's notoriously dangerous roads – are bicycles and motorcycles. Bicycles are fine on Formentera, but on Ibiza a motorcycle is much more convenient. Try hiring a motor scooter if there are two of you, or a mobylette (moped) if you want to drive solo. Mobylettes have a speed limit of 30kph at all times. Remember: crash helmets are compulsory in Spain.

Take Care

If you are driving in Ibiza be cautious. Apart from the main roads from Eivissa to the airport, Sant Antoni and Portinatx, roads are narrow, winding and poorly surfaced. And around the next corner there could be a herd of sheep or goats. The speed limits are 90kph (56mph), unless otherwise specified, on open roads and 50kph (31mph) in towns and villages.

The Weather

The Pine Islands have an enviable climate, with an average of 300 sunny days per year. During the summer you can almost guarantee 10 hours of sunshine daily. August is the hottest month with temperatures averaging 80°F (though midday temperatures can be much higher). Interestingly, throughout the year the temperature of the sea around the islands is the same, or just a little higher, than the average air temperature.

months races are generally held twice weekly. The races are held in the evening, usually finishing under floodlights.

Hippodromo Ibiza
✉ S'Hort Nou, Sant Rafel
☎ 908 16 24 03

Hippodromo Sant Jordi
✉ On the road from Eivissa to the airport, near Sant Jordi
☎ 39 66 69

Horse Riding

One of the best ways of seeing Ibiza, and one involving much less effort than walking or mountain biking, is from horseback. Specific tracks have been created to explore the wilder parts of the island and visitors can hire horses or join a trek to enjoy the exploration. A list of riding schools is given on page 110.

Live Music

Bar Pereira

A more conventional piano bar and therefore a more tolerable form of competition to the disco-vested interests (see below).
✉ 5 Calle Conde Rosellón, Eivissa ☎ 31 04 09

Las Dalias

There has been an off-season battle on Ibiza in recent times over the live music concerts held at Las Dalias, the discos claiming it is taking their custom. If the shows are still on they are worth the effort of seeing.
✉ At the 12km post on the main road near Sant Carles
☎ 33 50 42

Mountain Biking

Mountain bikes can be hired at most of the main towns and villages and these can be used to explore the green routes which have been specially created both on Ibiza and Formentera. On Ibiza a map is available from the Tourist Information Office giving details of available routes - ask for *Rutas en Mountain Bike*. The map also has details of specific itineraries near the larger towns. These itineraries even include a cross-section of the route so that cyclists can see the extent of climbing. The routes are long (between 25 and 45 kilometres) and some are very arduous.

On Formentera the Green Tours pamphlet gives details of 10 cycle/mountain bike itineraries, together with a further 9 walking routes. All these routes are short – distances range from 1 to 4 kilometres.

Nightclubs

There is a nightclub, with an excellent cabaret, in the Casino at Eivissa. The Casino also has a superb restaurant and a good pizzeria.

Sports Centres

Indoor tennis, squash, badminton etc are available at the following centres:

El Polideportivo Municipal de Eivissa
✉ Can Misses, Eivissa ☎ 31 35 64

El Polideportivo Municipal de Sant Antoni de Portmany
✉ Sant Antoni ☎ 34 54 02

Tennis
Many hotels have tennis courts, but you can also visit the following:

Ibizos Tennis Parc
✉ On road to Cala Llonga
☎ 33 92 56

Tennis Club
✉ Canaries, Eivissa
☎ 30 00 19

Tennis Sport Centre
✉ Caló d'en Real, Sant Josep
☎ 80 00 34

Walking
Ibiza and Formentera are ideal for walking. Much of the coast of Ibiza is followed by the Ruta de Falcó (see page 47). In addition to this 'long-distance' trail, all the major towns on Ibiza and the island of Formentera produce leaflets on walks in their areas. One that can be recommended is a long (23km) route that explores the uplands to the north of Sant Antoni, linking the town with Santa Agnès de Corona.

Watersports
Most of the islands' beaches have watersport equipment for hire. For those wishing to sail or windsurf, the following clubs will help.

Anfibios
✉ Platja d'en Bossa ☎ 908 26 99 77

CC Cats
✉ Platja se Ses Salines, Sant Jordi ☎ 908 63 06 32

Club Deportivo Ibiza Nueva
✉ Eivissa ☎ 31 20 01

Club Deportivo Marina Botafoch
✉ Eivissa ☎ 31 22 31

Club de Surf Ibiza
✉ Platja d'en Bossa
☎ 19 24 18

Club Maritimo Balear
✉ Platja Es Figueral
☎ 33 51 00

Club Náutico de Ibiza
✉ Eivissa ☎ 31 33 63

Club Náutico Sant Antoni
✉ Sant Antoni ☎ 34 06 45

Club Náutico Santa Eulària
✉ Sports Marina, Santa Eulària ☎ 908 26 85 95

Club Punta Arabí
✉ Platja Cala Martina, Es Canar ☎ 33 06 50

Escuela de Vela Cala Pada
✉ Club Cala Pada, Santa Eulària ☎ 33 08 86

Escuela de Vela y Windsurf Club Delfin
✉ Hotel Club Delfin, Cala Codolar ☎ 80 62 10

Hotel Es Pins
✉ Bahia de Sant Antoni
☎ 34 05 50

Puerto Deportivo Coralmar
✉ Cala Corral ☎ 34 21 10

Puerto Deportivo Ibiza
✉ Eivissa ☎ 31 06 11

Puerto Deportivo Santa Eulària
✉ Santa Eulària ☎ 33 97 54

Vela Náutica
✉ Platja Es Regueró, Sant Antoni ☎ 908 53 90 31

Vela Surf
✉ Cala de Sant Vicenç

Taxi Fares
At the head of Ibiza's taxis ranks is a board with the prices for destinations throughout the island. Consult this before you take a seat to avoid arguments at the end of your journey. Eivissa's taxi rank is in Paseo Vara de Rey.

What's On When

17 January
Festival of Sant Antoni in the town of Sant Antoni on Ibiza.

February
Carnival season on Ibiza. The main event is on 12 February at Santa Eulària.

Easter
Processions on Good Friday and Easter Sunday. Those to the cathedral in Dalt Vila are among the most impressive.

First Sunday in May
Procession of decorated wagons in Santa Eulària.

30 May
Festival of Sant Ferran in the village of the saint's name on Formentera.

24 June
Festival of Sant Joan, with bonfires and fireworks at many locations. Among the best festivals is that at La Mola, Formentera, with a bonfire kept alight through-out the year's shortest night.

16 July
Festival of La Virgen del Carmine (Our Lady of Carmen). The Virgin is the the patron saint of seafarers and there are parades of boats on both Ibiza (particularly in Eivissa's harbour) and Formentera (at La Savina). At the end of the procession the boats are blessed on the water.

25 July
Festival of San Jaime, the Patron Saint of Formentera. Festivals in all the island's towns and villages. The celebrations last for several days and include traditional *ball pages*.

5 August
Festival of Our Lady of the Snows, the Patron Saint of the Pine Islands. Celebrated all over the islands.

6 August -
As part of the Festival of Our Lady of the Snows Ibiza's corsairs are honoured with celebrations in Eivissa's harbour.

8 August
Festival of San Ciriaco, the patron saint of Eivissa. This coincides with another part of the Festival of Our Lady of the Snows when the Christian Reconquest of the island is celebrated with fireworks.

24 August
Festival in Sant Antoni with fireworks and bands to celebrate San Bartolome's Day.

8 September
Fiesta de Jesús, Santa Eulària. Chiefly religious but including traditional song and dance.

12 October
El Pilar, Formentera. A formal procession to the highest point on the island in honour of Our Lady of El Pilar.

1 November
All Saints' Day celebrations on both Ibiza and Formentera with the baking and eating of special cakes.

3 December
Bonfire and barbecue of pig meat in Plaça de la Iglesia, Sant Françesc de Formentera, to celebrate the patron saint's day.

Practical Matters

TIME DIFFERENCES

GMT 12 noon	Ibiza & Formentera 1PM	Germany 1PM	USA (NY) 7AM	Netherlands 1PM	Rest of Spain 1PM

BEFORE YOU GO

WHAT YOU NEED

- ● Required
- ○ Suggested
- ▲ Not required

	UK	Germany	USA	Netherlands	Spain
Passport/National Identity Card	●	●	●	●	▲
Visa	▲	▲	▲	▲	▲
Onward or Return Ticket	○	○	●	○	○
Health Inoculations	▲	▲	▲	▲	▲
Health Documentation (► 123, Health)	●	●	●	●	▲
Travel Insurance	○	○	○	○	○
Driving Licence (national with Spanish translation or International)	●	●	●	●	●
Car Insurance Certificate	●	●	●	●	○
Car Registration Document	●	●	●	●	○

WHEN TO GO

Ibiza

■■■ High season

☐ Low season

14°C	14°C	16°C	19°C	22°C	26°C	28°C	29°C	27°C	23°C	19°C	16°C
JAN	FEB	MAR	APR	MAY	JUN	JUL	AUG	SEP	OCT	NOV	DEC

 Wet   Cloud   Sun   Sunshine & showers

TOURIST OFFICES

In the UK
Spanish Tourist Office
22–3 Manchester Square
London W1M 5AP
☎ 0171 486 8077
Fax: 0171 486 8034

In the USA
Tourist Office of Spain
666 Fifth Avenue 35th
New York
NY 10103
☎ 212/265 8822
Fax: 212/265 8864

Tourist Office of Spain
8383 Wilshire Boulevard
Suite 960
Beverly Hills
Cal 90211
☎ 213/658 7188
Fax: 213/658 1061

POLICE (POLICÍA) 395861 (IBIZA); 322022 (FORMENTERA)

FIRE (BOMBEROS) 313033 (IBIZA)

AMBULANCE (AMBULÀNCIA) 397000 (IBIZA)

RED CROSS (CRUZ ROJA) 390303 (IBIZA)

WHEN YOU ARE THERE

ARRIVING

Spain's national airline, Iberia (☎ 901 333222), has scheduled flights to Ibiza's Es Codolar Airport from major Spanish and European cities, but most visitors arrive by charter flight. Formentera has no airport. There are ferry and hydrofoil services from the Spanish mainland to Ibiza.

Ibiza (Es Codolar) Airport Kilometres to Eivissa centre	Journey times	
	🚇	N/A
9 kilometres	🚌	15 minutes
	🚗	10 minutes

Ibiza Ferry Terminal In Eivissa centre	Journey times	
	🚇	N/A
	🚌	available
	🚗	available

MONEY

Spain's currency is the peseta, issued in notes of 1,000, 2,000, 5,000 and 10,000 pesetas and coins of 5, 10, 25, 50, 100, 200 and 500 pesetas. A one-peseta coin still exists but most bills are rounded down to the nearest 5 pesetas.

Traveller's cheques are accepted by most hotels, shops and restaurants in lieu of cash, but the rate of exchange may be less favourable than in banks. Traveller's cheques in pesetas are the most convenient.

Banks can be found in most towns or resorts in Ibiza and Formentera and handle traveller's cheques, Eurocheques and give advances on credit cards.

TIME

Like the rest of Spain, Ibiza and Formentera are one hour ahead of Greenwich Mean Time (GMT+1), but from late March until late September, summer time (GMT+2) operates.

CUSTOMS

 YES

Goods Obtained Duty Free Inside the EU or Goods Bought Outside the EU (Limits):
Alcohol (over 22° vol): 1L *or*
Alcohol (not over 22° vol): 2L *and* Still table wine: 2L
Cigarettes: 200 *or*
Cigars: 50 *or*
Tobacco: 250gms
Perfume: 50gms
Toilet water: 250ml
Goods Bought Duty and Tax Paid Inside the EU (Guidance Levels):
Alcohol (over 22° vol): 10L *and*
Alcohol (not over 22° vol): 20L *and*
Wine (max 60L sparkling): 90L *and* Beer: 110L
Cigarettes: 800 *and*
Cigars: 200 *and* Tobacco: 1kg
Perfume: no limit
Toilet water: no limit
You must be 17 and over to benefit from tobacco and alcohol allowances.

 NO

Drugs, firearms, ammunition, offensive weapons, obscene material, unlicensed animals.

UK
☎ 301818

Germany
☎ 315763

USA
☎ 722660
(Palma, Mallorca)

Netherlands
☎ 300450

WHEN YOU ARE THERE

TOURIST OFFICES

Ibiza and Formentera

● Consell Insular de Ibiza y
  Formentera
  Calle Bes 9
  Eivissa 07800
  ☎ 195900
  Fax: 195910

Ibiza

● Fomento del Turismo de
  Ibiza
  Historiador José Clapés 4
  Eivissa 07800
  ☎ 302490
  Fax: 302262

● Oficina de Información
  Turística de Ibiza
  Paseo Vara de Rey 13
  Eivissa 07800
  ☎ 301900
  Fax: 301562

● Oficina de Información
  Turística Municipal
  Santa Eulària
  Mariano Riquer Wallis s/n
  Eivissa 07840
  ☎ 330728
  Fax: 332959

● Oficina de Información
  Turística Sant Antoni
  Passeig de Ses Fonts s/n
  Eivissa 07820
  ☎ 343363
  Fax: 344175

Formentera

● Oficina de Información
  Turística Municipal
  Formentera
  Port de la Savina
  Formentera 07870
  ☎ 322057
  Fax: 322825

NATIONAL HOLIDAYS

J	F	M	A	M	J	J	A	S	O	N	D
2		(1)	(1)	1(2)	(1)	1	1		1	1	3

1 Jan	New Year's Day
6 Jan	Epiphany
Mar/Apr	Good Friday, Easter Monday
1 May	Labour Day
May/June	Corpus Christi
25 Jul	Saint James' Day
15 Aug	Assumption of the Virgin
12 Oct	National Day
1 Nov	All Saints' Day
6 Dec	Constitution Day
8 Dec	Feast of the Immaculate Conception
25 Dec	Christmas Day

Shops, banks and offices close on these days but in
the main resorts many places remain open.

OPENING HOURS

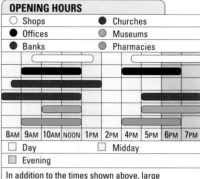

○ Shops	● Churches
● Offices	◐ Museums
● Banks	◐ Pharmacies

| 8AM | 9AM | 10AM | NOON | 1PM | 2PM | 4PM | 5PM | 6PM | 7PM |

□ Day   □ Midday
■ Evening

In addition to the times shown above, large
department stores, as well as supermarkets and
shops in tourist resorts may open outside these times,
especially in summer. In general, pharmacies, banks
and shops close on Saturday afternoon, though banks
stay open until 4:30PM Monday to Thursday, October
to May, but close Saturday, June to September.

The opening times of museums is just a rough guide;
some are open longer hours in summer while hours
are reduced in winter. Some museums close at
weekends or another day in the week.

DRIVE ON THE RIGHT

TOILETS FREE

PUBLIC TRANSPORT

Internal-island Flights Iberia operates several flights a day between Mallorca and Ibiza (flight time: 30 minutes). There are no direct flights from Menorca to Ibiza (you are routed via Mallorca). You must book ahead at the height of summer. Iberia's office on Ibiza is at Paseo Vara de Rey 15 (☎ 302580). For airport information: ☎ 300300. There is no airport on Formentera.

Buses If you want to explore and to mingle with the natives, hop on a bus (*autobús*). On Ibiza, there is a good service (around every half hour in summer) between Eivissa, Sant Antoni, Santa Eulària, Portinatx and a few larger beaches. On Formentera, buses only connect settlements along the main island road plus a few larger resorts, and timetables are not always adhered to. Always check the time of the last bus home.

Ferries Formentera can be reached by ferry or hydrofoil from Ibiza. It is only 11 nautical miles from Eivissa to La Savina but strong currents ensure the journey by ferry is slow (over an hour) and can be rough; the hydrofoil takes 30 minutes but is less enjoyable. During the summer there are ten sailings a day (six at other times) operated by Trasmediterránea (☎ 315100).

Urban Transport Only Eivissa is large enough to have its own transport system with a web of bus services linking the town centre with the suburbs and nearby beaches. Buses depart from the bus station (*estación de autobuses*) on Isidoro Macabich or from opposite the Delagación del Gobierno building further down the same avenue.

CAR RENTAL

The leading international car rental companies are represented at Ibiza airport and in the main towns and resorts. Many local companies offering competitive rates which should be considered. A hire car is essential for reaching those out-of-the-way coves.

TAXIS

Taxis can be hired at ranks (fares are fixed and displayed on a board), or phone (Eivissa ☎ 307000, Santa Eulària ☎ 330063; Sant Antoni ☎ 340074 /341721). Taxis are cheap and popular on Formentera; there are ranks at La Savina, Sant Francesc and Es Pujols.

DRIVING

There are no motorways on Ibiza or Formentera.

Speed limits on main roads: **100kph**
Speed limits on minor roads: **90kph**

Speed limits on urban roads: **50kph**

Must be worn in front seats at all times and in rear seats where fitted.

Random breath-testing. Limit: 80 micrograms of alcohol in 100ml of breath.

Fuel (*gasolina*) is available in four grades: *Super Plus* (98 octane), *Super* (96 octane) and often unleaded (*sin plomo*), *Mezcla* or *Normal* (90 octane), and *gasoleo* or *gasoil* (diesel). Petrol stations are normally open 6AM–10PM, and closed Sundays, though larger ones (often self service) are open 24 hours. Most take credit cards. There are few petrol stations in rural areas.

If you break down driving your own car and are a member of an AIT-affiliated motoring club, you can call the Real Automóvil Club de España (☎ 91 593 3333). If the car is hired follow the instructions given in the documentation; most of the international rental firms provide a rescue service.

PERSONAL SAFETY

The national police force, the Policía Nacional (brown uniforms) keep law and order in urban areas. Some resorts have their own tourist-friendly Policía Turística. If you need a police station ask for *la comisaría*.

To help prevent crime:

- Do not carry more cash than you need.
- Do not leave valuables on the beach or poolside.
- Beware of pickpockets in markets, tourist sights or crowded places.
- Avoid walking alone in dark alleys at night.

Police assistance:
☎ **091**
from any call box

TELEPHONES

A public telephone (*teléfono*) takes 25, 100 and 500-peseta coins (both new and old). Phonecards (*credifone*), from post offices and *tabacos*, cost 1,000 or 2,000 pesetas. All telephone numbers in the Balearic Islands have the code 971, so within Ibiza and Formentera you need dial only the six-figure numbers shown in this guide. To call the operator dial 002.

International Dialling Codes

From Ibiza and Formentera (Spain) to:

UK:	**07 44**
Germany:	**07 49**
USA:	**07 1**
Netherlands:	**07 31**

POST

Post Offices
Post offices (*correus*) are open as below but some also open in the afternoon and on Saturday morning. The main post office in Eivissa is at Calle Madrid 21, and on Formentera at Plaça Constitució 1, Sant Francesc.
Open: 9AM–2PM (Mon–Fri)
☎ 311380 (Ibiza)
☎ 322243 (Formentera)

ELECTRICITY

The power supply in Ibiza and Formentera is: 220–225 volts.

Sockets accept two-round-pin-style plugs, so an adaptor is needed for most non-Continental appliances and a transformer for appliances operating on 100–120 volts.

TIPS/GRATUITIES

Yes ✓ No ✗		
Restaurants (if service not included)	✓	10%
Cafés/bars (if service not included)	✓	change
Tour guides	✓	100ptas
Hairdressers	✓	change
Taxis	✓	10%
Chambermaids	✓	100ptas
Porters	✓	100ptas
Theatre/cinema usherettes	✓	change
Cloakroom attendants	✓	change
Toilets	✗	

PHOTOGRAPHY

What to photograph: archaeological monuments, secluded coves (*calas*), unspoiled fishing villages, the old town area of Eivissa.

Best time to photograph: the Ibizan summer sun can be powerful at the height of the day making photos taken at this time appear 'flat'; it is best to photograph in the early morning or late evening.

Where to buy film: film and camera batteries are readily available from tourist shops and *droguerías*.

HEALTH

Insurance

Nationals of EU and certain other countries can get medical treatment in Spain with the relevant documentation (Form E111 for Britons), although private medical insurance is still advised and is essential for all other visitors.

Dental Services

Dental treatment is not usually available free of charge as all dentists practice privately. A list of *dentistas* can be found in the yellow pages of the telephone directory. Dental treatment should be covered by private medical insurance.

Sun Advice

The sunniest (and hottest) months are July and August with an average of 11 hours sun a day and daytime temperatures of 29°C. Particularly during these months you should avoid the midday sun and use a strong sunblock.

Drugs

Prescription and non-prescription drugs and medicines are available from pharmacies (*farmàcias*), distinguished by a large green cross. They are able to dispense many drugs which would be available only on prescription in other countries.

Safe Water

Tap water is generally safe though it can be heavily chlorinated. Mineral water is cheap to buy and is sold as *con gaz* (carbonated) and *sin gaz* (still). Drink plenty of water during hot weather.

CONCESSIONS

Students/Youths Ibiza and Formentera are favourite destinations of the trendy young and latter-day hippies. The best holiday deals are available on a package tour rather than booking independently and Sant Antoni is the swinging heart of package-tour Ibiza. There are no specific concessions for students but if you hold an International Student Identity Card (ISIC), take it with you because it just may entitle you to a discount.

Senior Citizens Ibiza and Formentera are not obvious destinations for older travellers, but in winter when the resorts are quieter, hotels can offer economical long-stay rates. Otherwise there are no specific concessions for the older visitor.

CLOTHING SIZES

Ibiza/Formentera (Spain)	UK	Rest of Europe	USA	
46	36	46	36	Suits
48	38	48	38	
50	40	50	40	
52	42	52	42	
54	44	54	44	
56	46	56	46	
41	7	41	8	Shoes
42	7.5	42	8.5	
43	8.5	43	9.5	
44	9.5	44	10.5	
45	10.5	45	11.5	
46	11	46	12	
37	14.5	37	14.5.	Shirts
38	15	38	15	
39/40	15.5	39/40	15.5	
41	16	41	16	
42	16.5	42	16.5	
43	17	43	17	
34	8	34	6	Dresses
36	10	36	8	
38	12	38	10	
40	14	40	12	
42	16	42	14	
44	18	44	16	
38	4.5	38	6	Shoes
38	5	38	6.5	
39	5.5	39	7	
39	6	39	7.5	
40	6.5	40	8	
41	7	41	8.5	

WHEN DEPARTING

● Remember to contact the airport on the day prior to leaving to ensure the flight details are unchanged.

● If travelling by ferry you must check in no later than the time specified on the ticket.

● Spanish customs officials are usually polite and normally willing to negotiate.

LANGUAGE

The language that you hear on the streets is most likely to be Ibicenco, a version of Catalan, which itself shares features with both French and Spanish but sounds nothing like either and is emphatically a language, not a dialect. Catalan and Spanish both have official status on Ibiza and Formentera, and though Spanish will certainly get you by (it is still the language used by Ibizencos to address strangers), it is useful to know some Catalan if only to understand all those street signs which are being slowly replaced in Catalan. Below are some words of Ibicenco.

hotel	*hotel*	chambermaid	*cambrera*
bed and breakfast	*llit i berenar*	bath	*bany*
single room	*habitació senzilla*	shower	*dutxa*
double room	*habitació doble*	toilet	*toaleta*
one person	*una persona*	balcony	*balcó*
one night	*una nit*	key	*clau*
reservation	*reservas*	lift	*ascensor*
room service	*servei d'habitació*	sea view	*vista al mar*

bank	*banc*	credit card	*carta de crèdit*
exchange office	*oficina de canvi*	exchange rate	*tant per cent*
post office	*correus*	comission	*comissió*
coin	*moneda*	charge	
banknote	*bitllet de banc*	cashier	*caixer*
cheque	*xec*	change	*camvi*
travellers'	*xec de viatge*	foreign currency	*moneda*
cheque			*estrangera*

café	*cafè*	starter	*primer plat*
pub/bar	*celler/bar*	main course	*segón plat*
breakfast	*berenar*	dessert	*postres*
lunch	*dinar*	bill	*cuenta*
dinner	*sopar*	beer	*cervesa*
table	*taula*	wine	*vi*
waiter	*cambrer*	water	*aigua*
waitress	*cambrera*	coffee	*cafè*

aeroplane	*avió*	single ticket	*senzill-a*
airport	*aeroport*	return ticket	*anar i tornar*
train	*tren*	non-smoking	*no fumar*
bus	*autobús*	car	*cotxe*
station	*estació*	petrol	*gasolina*
boat	*vaixell*	bus stop	*la parada*
port	*port*	how do I get to...?	*per anar a...?*
ticket	*bitllet*	where is...?	*on és...?*

yes	*si*	you're welcome	*de res*
no	*no*	how are you?	*com va?*
please	*per favor*	do you speak	*parla anglès?*
thank you	*gràcies*	English?	
welcome	*de res*	I don't	*no ho entenc*
hello	*hola*	understand	
goodbye	*adéu*	how much?	*quant es?*
good morning	*bon dia*	open	*obert*
good afternoon	*bona tarda*	closed	*tancat*
goodnight	*bona nit*	today	*avui*
excuse me	*perdoni*	tomorrow	*demà*

Acknowledgements
The Automobile Assocation wishes to thank the following photographers, libraries and associations for their assistance in the preparation of this book:

MARY EVANS PICTURE LIBRARY 10, 14a
MRI BANKER'S GUIDE TO FOREIGN CURRENCY 119
NATURE PHOTOGRAPHERS LTD 12a (S C Bisserot), 13a (A J Cleave)
PICTURES COLOUR LIBRARY F/c (b) ceramics
R G SALE 21, 22, 25, 35, 44, 47, 53, 66, 68, 75, 79, 80, 82, 83, 86, 87, 89a
SPECTRUM COLOUR LIBRARY 7, 8, 40, 41, 88, 117a
WORLD PICTURES F/c (c), 5b, 23, 27a, 57b, 59, 81, 84, 85

The remaining photographs are held in the Association's own library (**AA PHOTO LIBRARY**) and were taken by JAMES TIMMS with the exception of the following:
KEN PATTERSON 122a, 122b
WYN VOYSEY B/c, 43, 60

Contributors
Copy editor: Rebecca Snelling   Page Layout: Design 23   Verifier: Pip Leahy
Researcher (Practical Matters): Colin Follett   Indexer: Marie Lorimer

Dear Essential Traveller

**Your comments, opinions and recommendations are very
important to us. So please help us to improve our travel
guides by taking a few minutes to complete this simple
questionnaire.**

*You do not need a stamp (unless posted outside the UK). If you do not want to cut this page
from your guide, then photocopy it or write your answers on a plain sheet of paper.*

Send to: **The Editor, AA World Travel Guides,
FREEPOST SCE 4598, Basingstoke RG21 4GY.**

Your recommendations...

We always encourage readers' recommendations for restaurants, nightlife
or shopping – if your recommendation is used in the next edition of the
guide, we will send you a *FREE* AA *Essential* **Guide** of your choice.
Please state below the establishment name, location and your reasons
for recommending it.

_____

_____

_____

_____

Please send me **AA *Essential*** _____
(*see list of titles inside the front cover*)

About this guide...

Which title did you buy?
    AA *Essential* _____
Where did you buy it? _____
When? m m / y y

Why did you choose an AA *Essential* Guide? _____

_____

_____

_____

_____

Did this guide meet your expectations?
    Exceeded ☐   Met all ☐   Met most ☐   Fell below ☐
    Please give your reasons_____

_____

_____

_____

continued on next page...

Were there any aspects of this guide that you particularly liked? _____
_____
_____
_____

Is there anything we could have done better? _____
_____
_____
_____
_____

About you…

Name (*Mr/Mrs/Ms*) _____
    Address _____
_____
_____ Postcode _____
Daytime tel nos _____

Which age group are you in?
Under 25 ☐ 25–34 ☐ 35–44 ☐ 45–54 ☐ 55–64 ☐ 65+ ☐

How many trips do you make a year?
Less than one ☐ One ☐ Two ☐ Three or more ☐

Are you an AA member? Yes ☐ No ☐

About your trip…

When did you book? m m / y y   When did you travel? m m / y y
How long did you stay? _____
Was it for business or leisure? _____
Did you buy any other travel guides for your trip?
    If yes, which ones? _____
_____

Thank you for taking the time to complete this questionnaire. Please send
    it to us as soon as possible, and remember, you do not need a stamp
    (*unless posted outside the UK*).

Happy Holidays!